When Kids Are Touched by Crisis

Les Christie
Randy Petersen

David C. Cook Publishing Co. Elgin, Illinois—Weston, Ontario

First Aid for Youth Groups
When Kids Are Touched by Crisis

Published by
David C. Cook Publishing Co.
850 N. Grove Ave., Elgin, IL 60120
Cable address: DCCOOK
Illustrations by Bill Duca
Design by Randy Maid
Printed in U.S.A.
ISBN: 1-55513-516-1

FirstAid FOR YOUTH GROUPS

When Kids Are Touched by Crisis

About the Authors 4

Does Your Group Need First Aid? 5

In Times of Crisis 6

Session 1: **Death** 9

Session 2: **Suicide** 17

Session 3: **Accident/Natural Disaster** 25

Session 4: **Racial Incident** 31

Session 5: **Church Split** 41

Session 6: **Scandal Involving a Christian Leader** 47

Session 7: **Pregnant Teen** 55

Session 8: **Divorce** 65

Session 9: **Arrest of a Friend** 73

Session 10: **Terminal Illness** 81

Session 11: **Terrorism/Murder** 87

Session 12: **Economic Depression** 93

Session 13: **National or International Incident** 101

Session 14: **Crime** 109

Session 15: **World Hunger** 117

About the Authors

Les Christie is a veteran youth worker and speaker. He serves as Minister of Youth at Eastside Christian Church in Fullerton, California, and has written several books and articles on youth ministry, including *When You Have to Draw the Line* (SonPower) and *Unsung Heroes* (Zondervan).

Les wrote the "In Times of Crisis" article for this book.

Randy Petersen is a freelance writer living in Westville, New Jersey. Formerly the executive editor of *Evangelical Newsletter* and *The Bible Newsletter*, he has also worked with young people and written curriculum for youth and adults.

Randy wrote sessions 1-15 of this book.

Does Your Group Need First Aid?

Wise is the youth worker who heeds this rule: "Expect the unexpected."

Whether they're as intensely personal as an eating disorder or as far away as a famine . . . whether they're as "minor" as a question about rock music or as devastating as a suicide . . . problems, questions, attitudes, and crises will arise that disrupt the life of your group.

Is it really possible to prepare for such disruptions? Now it is—with "First Aid for Youth Groups."

Each book in the "First Aid for Youth Groups" series is designed to help you respond quickly to specific issues, situations, and events that affect your group.

With the practical, biblical advice contained in each session, you'll be able to help your group members handle and learn from such crises as an accident or natural disaster, a terminal illness, or a teen's pregnancy. You'll be ready to respond to group members' questions as to whether a Christian can be gay or why God could allow good people to go to hell. You'll be prepared to address specific reasons for group apathy or immaturity. And you'll be able to help group members deal with such personal hurts as sexual abuse and physical impairment.

Created with the help of veteran youth workers, these sessions do more than address the problems and crises affecting individuals in your group. They're also designed to raise the sensitivity of other group members, and to cause the group itself to be an instrument of healing.

No one can solve serious problems with a meeting or two. But with "First Aid for Youth Groups," you can be ready with immediate help when symptoms appear. The prescription: Pick sessions as needed and apply the wisdom of God's Word directly to your group.

— Randy Southern, Series Editor

In Times of Crisis

One seasoned Christian leader has said that "some great crunch is almost inevitable in every pastor's life. It would have been helpful to me if, early in my ministry, I had known that and understood the diversity of emotional, psychological, and spiritual catastrophes." With *When Kids Are Touched by Crisis,* you, as a youth leader, have a tool to address the diversity of catastrophes in your group members' lives.

People establish religious convictions during crisis situations. So, in times of crisis, you have an incredible opportunity to help young people become Christians or become stronger in their faith. The danger in this situation is obvious: to mishandle or incorrectly advise a young person in a crisis situation can establish an anti-Christian ideology that can last a lifetime.

A crisis is an event that speeds up the heartbeat, lowers skin temperature, and makes your hands sweat. The one common denominator, the one thread that ties people together during a crisis is the fact that intense emotions are played out. Anger, anxiety, betrayal, confusion, guilt, fear, discouragement, and sorrow are all feelings that envelop and paralyze people during a crisis.

The cause of the crisis may involve the loss of someone or something significant, such as a loved one, a job, a girlfriend, a prized possession, or one's self-esteem. A sudden shift in one's role or status, or the appearance of new, threatening people or events may also trigger a crisis.

Crisis: No Respecter of Persons

You never know when crisis will strike. On a personal level, my family experienced a crisis on Wednesday, April 18, 1990. My nine-year-old son David was taken hostage at gunpoint on his school playground. A distraught woman held my son for 35 minutes as members of a police SWAT team assumed their positions. Fortunately, the drama had a happy ending as my son talked himself out of danger and negotiated his own release. He ended up on several local and national television programs looking like a hero. As his parents, we were just glad he was OK.

Young people in your ministry are in crisis. They are rich, poor, educated, uneducated, black, white, rural, urban, with no parents, with one parent, with two parents or more—in other words, just about anybody. The majority tend to hide their pain and despair; they most often go unnoticed.

The Ingredients of a Crisis

There are at least two different types of crises addressed in *When Kids Are Touched by Crisis.* One type is the result of our freedom as human beings. These are the moral/interpersonal crises—crises caused by our own decisions—such as being arrested for driving under the influence of alcohol. The other type of crisis is the result of "natural" disaster, such as an earthquake, a flood, and or the unexpected death of a loved one.

There are two ingredients to every crisis: the event itself and the decision on how to respond to the event. Every crisis, regardless of its origin, needs a decisive act as its second half. When a crisis occurs, you must help your group members concentrate on deciding, "What do I do now?" rather than "Who shall I blame?" This puts the major emphasis on present-tense problem solving.

As Christians facing crisis, your group members need to know that the Lord is with them. Right at the heart of the crisis, where the hard choices are being made, they have the living presence of Jesus Christ—not as One who takes away their choices, but as the Lord of freedom who enlarges the possibilities of their choices.

As a leader, one very important tool to have at your fingertips during a crisis situation is a comprehensive referral system. Knowing who to call not only enhances the possibility of addressing the crisis, but adds to your peace of mind. Make sure you have these names and phone numbers listed in an easily accessible place:

- Drug and alcohol-abuse hotline
- Rape, incest, and child abuse hotline
- Marriage, family, and child counselor
- Psychologist and/or psychiatrist
- Social worker
- Police department
- Hospitals and emergency rooms.

Interestingly, though crises are certainly not sought, they, at times, do bring positive results. Psalm 119:71 says, "It was good for me to be afflicted so that I might learn your decrees."

Crisis will probably always carry a negative connotation; however, it is good to remember that crisis often precedes a positive, critical breakthrough. Crises can reorder our lives, purify our motivations, and remind us again of the essence of ministry: to live honorably before God and to invite others to do the same. To be involved is to love, to risk, and to struggle. To be involved is to minister.

— Les Christie

Session 1

When someone dies, the effects ripple out to everyone who knew him or her. Obviously, those closest feel the most intense grief. The anguish is greater if the one who died was young, or if he or she died suddenly. We Christians mourn most for the person who was not, as far as we know, a Christian. Such deaths bring serious questions, serious pain, and serious self-examination.

Any counselor, youth worker, or caring friend must realize this: Grief is a process. Young people, like adults, naturally feel shock, anger, guilt, denial, and/or fear. As they go through the process, they eventually (1) accept the reality of the death; (2) honestly experience their own pain; (3) adjust to life without the deceased person; and (4) reinvest their emotions in others. Problems occur when kids get stuck within one of these steps. But it takes time to work through grief. Well-meaning friends do not help the mourner when they try to rush things.

A crisis like the death of a loved one can short-circuit a young person's spiritual growth—or it can rewire it and provide new energy. Genuine, sensitive, and intelligent caring is vital.

Crisis #1: Death

Specific Aims

- To help group members voice their own fears about death; to help them move forward in the grief process; and to reassure them that, for Christians, death means immediate, eternal life with Christ.

Scriptural Support

- Genesis 2:16, 17; 37:31-35
- II Samuel 18:31–19:8
- Ecclesiastes 3:1-4; 9:10
- John 3:16; 5:24; 11:25, 26
- Romans 6:23
- Philippians 1:21-23
- I Timothy 6:12, 17-19
- Hebrews 2:14, 15; 9:27, 28
- Revelation 14:13

Special Preparation

- Bibles
- Copies of Student Sheet 1-A ("How I Feel")
- Copies of Student Sheet 1-B ("Life and Death")
- Pencils
- Chalkboard and chalk or newsprint and marker

1 Life and Death

If there has been a recent tragedy prompting this session, your students may arrive in a somber mood. Some may be cracking inappropriate jokes or acting silly as a way of releasing tension. Remember that not all students deal with death at the same level. Be sensitive to group members' feelings. Open the meeting with something like this:

We are going to be talking today about death. A lot of us have been deeply affected by the recent news about ________. You may have questions about death. You probably have a lot of feelings inside, and you're not sure if they're right or wrong. Today, we want to talk as openly as we can about our thoughts and feelings. Only by being honest can we truly deal with this.

I don't expect that this session will answer all of your questions or make everything all better. But it should help sort some things out for you.

If this session is not in response to a recent tragedy, begin by asking, **If you were to describe death to a six year old, what would you say?** Ask if anyone has ever experienced the death of a loved one. Call on one or two volunteers who have lost a loved one to share their experience.

2 How I Feel

Distribute copies of Student Sheet 1-A ("How I Feel") and pencils. Give group members a few minutes to fill out the sheet. Assure them that you will not collect these papers (but you will allow anyone who wants to, to talk about these feelings).

After everyone has finished this activity, begin the discussion. Start by saying: **Each of these statements is something that has been felt—and fairly often—by people dealing with grief over the death of a loved one. They are very normal feelings to have at such times. It's not wrong to have feelings like these. It may be unhealthy to keep having some of these feelings six months or a year from now. But right now they are normal, understandable, and OK. So let's talk about them.**

Read the first statement on the student sheet and ask if there is anyone who circled the 3 ("very strongly") for it. Invite group members to elaborate, but don't push. If discussion is brewing, allow it to continue. (In fact, you may want to devote the whole session to allowing group members to get their feelings out, and pick up with the Bible study section next time.) If group members don't want to talk, stop after the first three and ask if there is any statement that really struck a chord with someone. Practice sensitivity here. Look for expressions that indicate a person wants to speak. If there's no discussion, move on.

If you think it's appropriate, you may want to share the following with your group members. If not, use the information for your own background as you prepare the session.

Elisabeth Kubler-Ross has studied the psychological processes of people who are dying and their families. She found five steps that families regularly go through when dealing with death. They are: (1) *Denial*—it didn't really happen, it's all a dream; (2) *Anger*, at self, the deceased, and God; (3) *Bargaining*, with God; (4) *Depression*, examining your own life, purpose, helplessness, etc.; (5) *Resolution*, finally learning to live without the deceased.

All healthy people go through most of these steps, or something like them, though not necessarily in this order.

3 Good Grief

Ask group members to turn to Genesis 37:31-35. Have someone read it aloud. Remind the group briefly about the story of Joseph and his brothers: Joseph's brothers ganged up on him and sold him as a slave; then they tried to make Jacob, their father, think the boy had died.

Ask: **How did Jacob mourn for his son?** (He tore his clothes and wore sack-cloth. This was the common custom in those days, sort of like wearing black to a funeral today.)

How long did Jacob mourn? (Many days.)

Why do you think Jacob "refused to be comforted"? Can you relate to this feeling? (Apparently, his grief was very strong, stronger than that of other family members. He probably felt they didn't understand his grief.)

Jacob said, "In mourning will I go down to the grave to my son." What did he mean by this? How would you put that in modern words? ("Life's not worth living without my son. I might as well die. I should have died in place of him, so I will mourn myself to death.") **Have you ever felt this way?**

Have the group turn to II Samuel 18:31. Before it is read, explain the story: Absalom has led a revolt against his father, King David. Absalom has just been killed in battle, and a messenger has hurried back to give David what he thinks will be good news.

Ask someone to read verses 31-33 aloud. Ask: **What was the king's first concern when he heard the news of the battle?** (Absalom's safety.)

How did the king respond when he heard that Absalom was dead? (He was shaken.)

Why wasn't David rejoicing in the victory over this rebel? (The rebel was his son.)

Can you understand the feeling when David says, "If only I had died instead of you"? Have you ever felt like that?

Have someone else read aloud II Samuel 19:1-8. Ask: **How did the soldiers respond to David's grieving?** (They were probably confused. They had won a great battle, but the king was unhappy about it. They probably expected a victory parade. Instead they "stole into the city" as if they had lost the battle.)

How many times in this passage is it recorded that David cried, "O Absalom, my son"? (Five, with a few extra "my son's.")

What does this indicate about David's grief? (It was strong. He obviously saw Absalom as his "son" and not just a rebel.)

Do you think David was overdoing it?

What did Joab (the army commander) have to say to David? Put this in your own words. (Stop mourning for this rebellious son and start paying attention to the loyal soldiers who won this battle for you. If you don't shape up, you're going to lose this war.)

Do you think Joab's comments were appropriate, or did they lack sensitivity?

What effect did these words have on David? (He got back to work.)

What would you have said to David had you been there?

Ask a volunteer to read aloud Ecclesiastes 3:1-4. Ask: **How does this passage apply to what Joab was telling David?** (Joab was saying, "There is a time to mourn, David, but now you have a war to fight.")

What does it tell us? (There is a time to mourn, but we can't spend so much time in our grief that we neglect our responsibilities, or the people around us who care about us.)

What do these verses tell you about grief? (Grief, sorrow, mourning are a part of life.)

If you think it's appropriate, share the following information with your group:

Jewish people have developed some great traditions to support the grieving process. In the days immediately following the funeral, there is the *Shivah*. Friends come and stay with the family several hours each evening, bringing food, helping with details of home life, or just being there. The word *Shivah* literally means "to sit," and that's the idea, just to sit with the grieving family and support them by your presence.

About six months to a year later—it differs depending on the family—there is the "unveiling." There is a brief ceremony with close family members, and it signals the official end of the mourning process.

The crucial thing about these traditions is that they allow time for the grieving to take place and for the healing to happen. There *is* a time to mourn—and we mustn't cut that short. There is also a time to stop mourning and go on with life.

4 Crossing the Line

Distribute copies of Student Sheet 1-B ("Life and Death"). Have group members form three groups. Assign each group the following Scripture passages.

Group A—Ecclesiastes 9:10; Hebrews 9:27, 28; Hebrews 2:14, 15; John 11:25, 26.

Group B—Genesis 2:16, 17; Romans 6:23; John 5:24; Revelation 14:13.

Group C—Philippians 1:21-23; John 3:16; I Timothy 6:12, 17-19.

Instruct the groups to read their assigned passages and answer these two questions:

What does this tell me about life and death?

How does this make me feel?

Give the groups several minutes to work. Then have a spokesperson for each group read the assigned verses and give the group's answers. Suggest that each group jot down notes from the other groups' presentations on their student sheets. You may wish to write key ideas on the board.

Use the following to supplement your discussion of the passages.

Group A

Ecclesiastes 9:10—A bleak view, but it reminds us of the "common wisdom" of our age: You only go around once in life, so grab all the gusto you can get.

Hebrews 9:27, 28—Death and judgment are inevitable, but Christ's sacrifice is available.

Hebrews 2:14, 15—We don't need to be afraid of death anymore. Christ has destroyed its power.

John 11:25, 26—We assure ourselves of life after death by believing in Jesus.

Group B

Genesis 2:16, 17—The penalty for disobeying God was death. [NOTE: The death of Adam and Eve was not immediate, but the processes of death began with their disobedience. Also, the spiritual "death" of separation from God began at that point.]

Romans 6:23—Sin brings death—physical death sometimes, but primarily spiritually. God gives life.

John 5:24—Jesus speaks of "crossing over" from death to life. That is, we live in the realm of death until we know Jesus. He changes everything.

Revelation 14:13—Because we are headed for heavenly rest, the death of Christians can be "blessed."

Group C

Philippians 1:21-23—Paul is torn because he realizes that death is a blessing, but he would also like to stay on earth and do God's work.

John 3:16—God's plan is for us to avert eternal death by believing in Jesus.

I Timothy 6:12, 17-19—We must "take hold of" eternal life, even as we live on earth.

How should we respond to the death of a believer? (It is natural to mourn, because our relationship with this person has been cut off for now. But we can also rejoice that the person has a new, more direct relationship with God.)

How should we respond to the death of an unbeliever? This is a tough question, because the Bible does not tell us what we want to hear. Point out that it's clear from Scripture that those who do not accept Christ as Savior face eternal punishment, death, and separation from God. We must respond with deep sorrow when an unbeliever dies, and we must redouble our efforts to bring others into a saving relationship with Jesus. The only bit of hope we can offer is that we don't know what happened in the person's soul in the moments before death. We know that God will mercifully hear a cry of faith at any moment.

How can we "take hold of" eternal life right now, and in the coming week? (Live with the power of Christ; get a heavenly perspective on things; let God's Spirit guide our priorities.)

5 Life Is . . .

Say something like: **During times when we're touched by death, we tend to think more about life. Our own ability to live becomes much more precious, much more scary, much more important. Let's try to put some of those feelings on paper. At the bottom of your student sheet, write your own epitaph—what would you like to have written on your tombstone after you die.**

Give group members a few minutes to do this, then ask if anyone would like to read his or her epitaph to the group. Be ready with an epitaph you've written for yourself.

Close in prayer, asking God for strength in dealing with this matter of death—and life. If appropriate, invite any group members who want to talk to you further about death and eternal life to meet with you later.

How I Feel

Indicate, on a scale of 0 to 3, how true these statements are of you. Circle the number:
0 - If you don't feel this way at all.
1 - If you feel this way a little bit.
2 - If you feel this way a "medium" amount.
3 - If you feel very strongly this way.

3 2 1 0 1. I miss someone close to me who died.

3 2 1 0 2. I am angry at this person for dying.

3 2 1 0 3. I feel guilty for not doing more for this person.

3 2 1 0 4. I am afraid that I may die soon, too.

3 2 1 0 5. I am afraid that other people I love will die soon.

3 2 1 0 6. I am worried about whether this person is in heaven.

3 2 1 0 7. I am beginning to wonder if there really is a heaven.

3 2 1 0 8. I feel like it's all a dream.

3 2 1 0 9. I feel this person's presence near me.

3 2 1 0 10. I think it's up to me to carry on what this person was doing.

3 2 1 0 11. I can't imagine what life will be like without this person.

3 2 1 0 12. I am afraid to get close to other people because they might leave me, too.

3 2 1 0 13. I feel physically sick over this.

3 2 1 0 14. What's the use? Life has no meaning anymore.

3 2 1 0 15. If I were a better person, maybe God would not have let this happen to me.

3 2 1 0 16. If I become a better person, maybe God will bring this person back.

3 2 1 0 17. I'm confused.

3 2 1 0 18. I wish someone would just hold me.

3 2 1 0 19. I'm sick and tired of everyone saying how sorry they are.

3 2 1 0 20. I feel very close to God because of this.

3 2 1 0 21. I'm afraid that I'm not mourning enough for this person.

3 2 1 0 22. I feel angry with God for letting this person die.

Life and Death

Group A

Ecclesiastes 9:10

Hebrews 9:27, 28

Hebrews 2:14, 15

John 11:25, 26

Group B

Genesis 2:16, 17

Romans 6:23

John 5:24

Revelation 14:13

Group C

Philippians 1:21-23

John 3:16

I Timothy 6:12, 17-19

Session 2

A suicide shakes you. If the victim was one of your own young people, you are probably asking yourself a million questions. "Why didn't I see it coming? What should I have done differently?"

Guilt will weigh you down. This is natural. Your "failed Messiah" complex may come out in full fury. Deal with it—perhaps by talking it out with a trusted senior minister or other confidant—and move on.

The advice is similar to what they tell parents on planes: Put the oxygen mask on first, then care for your children. If you are going down yourself, you're in no position to help your kids. Similarly, as you deal with a suicide in your group, you probably have more to deal with than your kids do. Make sure you have your own equilibrium before you walk through this with your kids.

Suicides are especially troublesome because the same person is seen as both criminal and victim. We don't know where to put our feelings. Sorrow, anger, guilt, fear—they all well up within us. The very thought that a person would choose to end this life offends us at a gut level. But some may find it strangely appealing.

The keys to this session are honesty and "ventilation." Let the crazy feelings be vented, but be sure that God's love and care are honestly presented as well.

Crisis #2: Suicide

Specific Aims

• To help group members deal with the conflicting emotions regarding suicide; to help them reaffirm their own reasons for living; and to help them acknowledge that God is with them always.

Scriptural Support

• Psalm 103:1-6, 8-18
• Isaiah 40:25-31
• Jeremiah 33:1-3

Special Preparation

• Bibles
• Copies of Student Sheet 2-A ("Pardon Me")
• Copies of Student Sheet 2-B ("When Things Get Tough")
• Pencils
• Chalkboard and chalk or newsprint and marker

[NOTE: Before leading this session, you may want to read over the material for the session on "Death." This will provide good background for you and may offer some activities or Scripture passages that could be used in this session.]

1 An Annoying Thought

If a suicide has occurred in your area recently, introduce the subject by saying something like: **We're going to talk today about a subject that scares most of us: suicide. The recent event** [a suicide in the area] **has made us all very sad, but it has also filled our minds with questions. Some of us feel angry, others guilty. It's hard to handle all these feelings.**

Ask everyone to try an experiment. **For the next thirty seconds, try not to think about a car.** Pause for thirty seconds. **Hard to do, wasn't it?**

There are two ways to deal with suicide. One is to ignore it and hope it will go away. But that usually doesn't work. The questions keep coming back and the pressure builds. It's annoying, like trying not to think about a car.

The better way to approach the subject of suicide is to talk about it, to discover why someone might reach such a low point, to see how we can keep ourselves from getting there, and to see how we can hang onto our friends. We have to be honest, and caring, and smart.

2 Debriefing

[NOTE: This section assumes that there has been a recent suicide, which serves as the focus for this meeting. If not, or, if the tragedy is so close that frank discussion would be painful, you might choose to reword the questions in general terms.]

Tell everyone that you're going to give a pop quiz. You'll read some statements, and ask group members to indicate if they think the statement is true or false.

1. More than 5,000 teenagers in the U. S. commit suicide every year.

2. The U.S. teenage suicide rate is higher than that of any other age group.

3. The U.S. has the highest suicide rate of any country in the world.

4. The most popular method of suicide among teens and college-aged young people is ingesting poison.

After you have read all of the statements, explain that *all* of the statements are false. The correct answers are:

1. About 2,000 teens commit suicide in the U.S. every year. Twenty million kids don't.

2. The suicide rate in the U.S. is higher for adults (highest for adults over the age of 50).

3. Austria, Canada, and Denmark have higher suicide rates.

4. The most popular method of suicide among teens and college-aged young people is by using firearms.

Ask: **Why do you think ________ (or, any person) committed suicide?** (To escape from problems or pressure; to relieve extreme guilt; to get attention; to get revenge; to avoid irrational fears; because of unrequited love; to remove a feeling of helplessness in other areas of life.)

What circumstances in this person's life might have contributed to the suicide? Do not let discussion of this question turn this into a gossip session.

If you had the power to go back in time and change one thing in this person's life, what do you think you would do? Do you think this would really make a difference?

How does this suicide make you feel right now? If you could say one thing to the suicide victim now, what would it be?

Conclude this section by saying something like: **The feelings you have just identified are all very normal, understandable feelings. You may be afraid that these feelings are "wrong" to have, that they're not "Christian," or that they're unhealthy. They're only unhealthy if you get stuck there—if you stop growing back to a state of health. Of course, you can always take any feelings you have to God. He will help you sort them out.**

3 Call Me

Have group members turn to Jeremiah 33:1-3. As they are finding the passage, introduce this Bible study section by saying something like: **As Christians we can be sure of two things: (1) God is in control; (2) God cares about us.** Write these two statements on the board.

Ask a volunteer to read aloud Jeremiah 33:1-3. Say: **Let's look at this backwards. Looking at verse 3, what does God ask us to do?** (To call on Him.)

What does He promise to do? (To answer; to tell us great things. The idea is that God has great things in store for us.)

Which of the two statements on the board does this seem to confirm? (God cares about us.)

Look at verse 2. How does God describe Himself? (The Creator, who formed and established the earth.)

Which of the two statements on the board does this seem to confirm? (God is in control.)

How does verse 2 connect with verse 3? (Because God is in control, He is able to help us when we need Him.)

Now to verse 1. Where was Jeremiah when God told him this? (Imprisoned, "confined.")

Why would Jeremiah need to hear this at that time? (He was helpless; he needed God's all-powerful help.)

When have you felt "confined," needing God to come and rescue you?

4 I Beg Your Pardon?

Distribute copies of Student Sheet 2-A ("Pardon Me"). Divide into three groups, assigning each group one of the Scripture passages on the sheet. Give the groups about 10 minutes to talk together about the questions listed. Then bring them back to discuss the passages.

Most of the questions are subjective or straight from the text, but here are a few comments that may help:

Psalm 103:1-6

"all my inmost being"—refers to the whole person, from the inside-out;

"the pit"—a reference to the grave, although it might be used figuratively for "down" times in life.

Psalm 103:8-18

"we are dust"—Adam was made from dust; God knows our frailty and does not expect more of us than we can do;

Isaiah 40:25-31

"stumble and fall"—the text makes clear that young people do stumble and fall, as part of our frail humanity; but by hoping in God, we can get up and run again;

"hope in the Lord"—essentially means to trust in Him, yet it has a strong leaning toward the future; expecting great things from God in the future gives us strength to soar above present problems.

5 Troubleshooting

Distribute copies of Student Sheet 2-B ("When Things Get Tough"). These are statements from people in trouble—people who might be thinking about suicide. Have volunteers read each of the quotes. After each one, ask:

If you were this person's best friend, what would you say to him or her?

What things would you recommend that this person do over the next week or month in order to improve the situation?

Have you ever felt like this? How did you escape?

Have the group members turn their student sheets over and write a heading at the top: "My Escape Strategy." Ask them to write, in 50 words or less, what they would want someone else to tell them or to do for them if they ever got *really* depressed.

If you have time, ask volunteers to read their responses to the group. Then ask group members to exchange sheets with a friend and use the information on their friends' sheets for future reference.

Point out that suicidal people usually feel there's "no way out"—but there's *always* a way out other than suicide. Invite group members to come to you to talk if they ever feel "trapped" or begin thinking that there's "no way out."

6 Litany of Hope

Ask everyone to stand in a circle with their arms on the shoulders of their neighbors. Close the session with a "Litany of Hope." You'll read a statement, and the group will respond by saying "Give us help, Lord."

Say: **We need each other.** (Give us help, Lord.)

We need to bear each other's burdens. (Give us help, Lord.)

We need to understand each other and forgive each other. (Give us help, Lord.)

We have to hang on to each other, and show others in our lives how important they are to us. (Give us help, Lord.)

We need to know You're with us, Lord. (Give us help, Lord.)

Have a "group hug" before leaving the circle.

Pardon Me

Group A
Psalm 103:1-6

1. How do these verses make you feel? Write down six words that describe your feelings.

2. When it says that "all my inmost being" praises God, what does that mean?

3. What does the Lord do for us?

4. Have you ever felt like you were in "the pit" (v. 4)? When?

5. Rewrite verse 6 in modern terms.

6. How could this passage help someone who was contemplating suicide?

Group B
Psalm 103:8-18

1. How do these verses make you feel? Write down six words that describe your feelings.

2. How is God described?

3. How does He deal with us when we do wrong?

4. Verse 14 says, "He remembers that we are dust." What does that mean in modern terms?

5. What does this say about God's love?

6. How could this passage help someone who was contemplating suicide?

Group C
Isaiah 40:25-31

1. Write down six words that describe the Lord's strength, according to this passage.

2. Have you ever felt like saying what is said in verse 27, as if God didn't know what was happening to you? When?

3. What does it mean to "hope in the Lord"?

4. What happens to those who "hope in the Lord"?

5. Does this mean that believers will never "stumble and fall"?

6. How could this passage help someone who was contemplating suicide?

When Things Get Tough

Jason

I guess my life was going OK, nothing special. But then I met Jennifer. I had never really dated anyone seriously before, but there she was. I was crazy about her, and she was crazy about me—at first. I wanted to spend more and more time with her. I thought about her all the time. I guess my grades slipped a little, and I sort of stopped hanging out with my friends, because when I wasn't with Jennifer, I was writing notes to her or buying something for her—you know.

I guess she got tired of me. She said she needed a break. We decided—well, she decided—we should stop seeing each other. And you know the story. I'd see her at school with her friends, and sometimes she'd be talking to a guy, and it would just rip my heart out.

If I can't have Jennifer, I don't want anything. She is my whole world. If she only knew how much I love her, she would know how perfect we are together. But every time I try to show her, she takes it wrong. She feels threatened, or something. I don't know what to do anymore. Maybe if I did something really big—if I wrote a suicide note—then she'd understand.

Cyndi

Yesterday was my birthday. Nothing happened. Mom worked late and Dad—well, Dad doesn't live with us anymore. He didn't even call. I came home looking for candles and cake, like when I was little. But, nope. I should have known.

Mom was all upset about it this morning. She said Dad was supposed to take me out to dinner yesterday, but he must have forgotten. Mom said she'd call him and yell at him. Once again they're fighting about me. It's not really me that they care about—they just want to hurt each other.

But, you know, if it weren't for me, they'd probably still be together. They wouldn't have anything to fight about. They'd be better off without me.

So, 16 years and one day old, I jam the headphones on and get lost in the beat. What else is there? I know where Mom keeps her pills. Maybe I could just drift off to sleep. Ha! It would be days before they realized I was gone.

Rachel

I don't know what to do.

I won't bore you with the details, but the basic thing is that, well, I had sex. That sounds so cold and clinical, but that's what it was. Not romantic at all. Met a guy at a party, got a little drunk, and next thing I knew, Little Miss Virgin was dead.

For most girls at school, this wouldn't be the end of the world, but you don't understand. Everything I've heard from Mom and Dad and everyone at church since I was a kid, was: "Keep yourself pure for that special someone." And I believed in that. I guess I still do.

But now I'm not "pure" anymore. And of course, the guy I did it with is the school blabbermouth, so it's only a matter of minutes before my parents hear the story on the evening news. Already, people at school and church are looking at me funny. "Oh, it's you, the former Good Girl."

I sat in church Sunday and nothing got through. I felt like such a hypocrite. Before, God was so important in my life. Now, it's like I pushed Him far away. Where can I turn? Mom and Dad would kill me. My church friends would be shocked. My school friends would laugh. If they only knew how bad I feel about this. If God only knew how ashamed I am. There's no way out, except . . .

Session 3

Easy answers fade in the face of tragedy. When an earthquake sandwiches unsuspecting drivers between concrete slabs; when a flood sweeps young lives away; when a drunk driver careens into the path of our star pupil—what do we say? We often try to throw theology at the nagging questions. Sometimes it helps, sometimes it doesn't.

Why does God allow such things to happen? To listen to modern philosophers, we seem to have a choice between a cruel God who plays tricks on us and a caring God who has lost control of His universe. Surely there is a better model.

We may never completely understand God's ways down here. They are beyond us. But we must still cling to Him; tragic events may shake many of our assumptions about God, but they must not sever our communication with Him.

As you lead this session, dare to admit that even *you* don't understand all that God does. Encourage group members to struggle with the hard questions and feelings raised by accidents and disasters. God is a wrestler, and those who wrestle with Him—Abraham, Jacob, David, Jeremiah—seem to know Him best.

CRISIS #3: ACCIDENT/NATURAL DISASTER

Specific Aims

• To help group members recognize that the powerful God who has complete control over all nature is also ready and willing to help us in our times of trouble; and to help them affirm that, no matter how random, devastating, and incomprehensible an incident may seem, God's hand will work through it.

Scriptural Support

• Genesis 18:20-33; 19:24
• Numbers 11:4-6, 10-15, 18-23
• Psalms 44:8-26; 74:1-11
• Jeremiah 20:7-10
• Luke 13:1-5
• Romans 11:33-36

Special Preparation

• Bibles
• Copies of Student Sheet 3-A ("Talking Back")
• Copies of Student Sheet 3-B ("What Does God Look Like?")
• Pencils
• Chalkboard and chalk or newsprint and marker

1 WHAT HAPPENED?

If a recent tragedy has occurred to prompt this session, ask volunteers to talk about the incident. If not, ask group members to think about natural tragedies that have occurred in their lifetime. What happened? Who was affected? How did this affect members of your group? How does the group feel about it?

Say: **When something affects us as deeply [as this event has], there is a tendency to shut down, to turn off our emotions, to get angry and to stew in our anger, or to get cynical and depressed. I challenge you all today to stay open. You have questions in your hearts; ask them. You have doubts about God; tell Him, or tell us. You have fears about the future; voice them. Only if we are honest with ourselves and each other can the healing begin.**

2 HONEST TO GOD

Distribute copies of Student Sheet 3-A ("Talking Back"). Say something like: **Are you mad—or have you ever been mad—at God? If so, you're in good company. Let's look at some scriptural examples of people who dared to talk back to God.**

Divide the group into five small groups. Assign each group one of the Scripture passages on the student sheet. Give everyone 8-10 minutes to fill out the sheets; then bring the group back together to talk it through.

Explain that some of the greatest heroes of the Bible had major complaints or struggles with God. They sometimes felt disappointed and used. God seemed unfair to them. And, in most cases, God did not scold them for disbelief. He often used their struggle to enhance their faith. And sometimes He was even convinced to do what they wanted.

Say: **We often have the idea that it's wrong to talk back to God, to tell Him how we feel. We think that if we were real Christians, we would never be disappointed or bothered or angry at God. And so, when a tragedy occurs, or when our lives begin to hurt, we feel guilty for these feelings, and that takes us even further away from God.**

But if Abraham and Moses and Jeremiah could talk back to God in terms like these, so can we. God wants us to keep talking to Him, even if we're confused or irked by what He's doing.

3 Picturing God

Distribute copies of Student Sheet 3-B ("What Does God Look Like?"). Give group members a minute or two to look over the pictures and fill in the blanks. Remind them that you want adjectives from the *heart*—not what they *think* is right, but what they *feel*. Assure them that there are no wrong answers.

Then go through the pictures one by one to see who chose what picture to represent God. Ask volunteers to share their list of adjectives and explain why each was chosen. Be ready with a few adjectives of your own.

4 The Toppling Tower

Say something like: **We know from the Bible that God is love. But God is also holy. He hates sin. You may be asking, "How can a loving God let tragedies happen?" But the Bible turns that around to ask, "How can a holy God allow human beings to continue in their sinful ways without bringing harsh judgment on them?"**

We may not like looking at it that way, but that may be because our understanding of God's love is too small. For instance, parents show love by buying their child an ice-cream cone, but also by grounding him for a week when he misbehaves. In the same way, our idea of God's love needs to be big enough to encompass His holiness, and to last through all eternity.

Have the group turn to Luke 13:1-5 and ask a volunteer to read it aloud. Explain that, apparently, some Galileans were massacred as they offered sacrifices in the temple. Also, a tower in Siloam fell and crushed 18 people.

Ask: **If you had been a family member or friend of the people who were killed in these events, how would you feel?** (The feelings would probably be the same as with any tragedy: denial, confusion, anger, etc.)

Did the people who died commit any special sins that brought the tragedy on them? (Apparently not. Jesus said they were not "more guilty" than others living in Jerusalem.)

What is Jesus' message to His hearers? (That they, too, deserve to die. They need to throw themselves on God's mercy to spare themselves.)

Point out that the phrase "more guilty" (vs. 4) indicates that the victims, like anyone else in the world, were guilty of sin. If it were not for God's mercy, none of us would be spared, all of us would die, and we'd all be separated from God forever. That's what we deserve.

We sometimes talk about the "innocent" victims of tragedy. True, the victim may have done nothing to bring on that specific tragedy, but no one is innocent in God's eyes.

5 Doxology

Have the group turn to Romans 11:33-36. Say: **In the middle of the Book of Romans, Paul faces some pretty tough questions—not physical tragedies, but spiritual tragedies. Why do people reject God and why does God let them? The answer seems to be wrapped up in the mysterious mercy of God. But even Paul doesn't understand it. Here's how he closes that section.**

Ask a volunteer to read these verses. Note that verses 33 and 34 indicate that we can't always understand God's ways. Verse 35, however, indicates that God doesn't owe us anything—He can do whatever He wants. Verse 36 says that He is still our Creator ("from Him"), sustainer ("through Him"), and future hope ("to Him")—in other words, we owe Him everything. The passage closes with a benediction, indicating that we can still praise God even when we don't understand what He's doing.

Post a large sheet of newsprint and have markers available. Announce to the group that you will now, together, write a psalm. Each group member will write a verse or two—if he or she wishes. Emphasize that psalms are not always full of praise and happiness; sometimes they contain complaints. But they always seem to tell God exactly how the writer feels.

Ask group members to think about what they'd like to write. When they're ready, have them add their verses to the newsprint. Point out that the verses don't necessarily have to go along with each other.

When all who wish to have contributed, read the entire psalm as a closing prayer, followed by Romans 11:33-36.

Talking Back

Scripture Passages
Group 1—Genesis 18:20-33; 19:24
Group 2—Numbers 11:4-6, 10-15, 18-23
Group 3—Psalm 44:8-26
Group 4—Psalm 74:1-11
Group 5—Jeremiah 20:7-10

Questions

1. Who is "talking back to God" in your passage?

2. What is he upset about?

3. In 25 words or less, summarize his complaint.

4. How would you describe his feelings at this point?

5. Have you ever felt like this? When?

6. Did this person's complaint change anything? What? [You may need to consult some surrounding verses.]

7. Do you think this complaint improved or worsened this person's relationship with God?

WHAT DOES GOD LOOK LIKE?

Circle the picture that comes closest to your idea of God. Place a check mark beside the image that most kids your age have of God.

Loving Grandfather

Terrorist

Brilliant Business Executive

Mad Scientist

Pal

Prankster

Hassled Schoolteacher

Strict Principal

On the lines below, list five words that you might use to describe God right now. Don't just say what you think is right, say how you feel.

Session 4

Vandals paint swastikas on a synagogue. African-American kids attack a Korean shop in their neighborhood. White kids bait and chase a black teen to his death.

The headlines scream to us that something is wrong, very wrong, with our society. Somehow, on the road to a world of love and unity, we got detoured, and fell among thieves.

The good news is that most of your kids probably have grown up with a doctrine of racial equality taught in schools. But the bad news is that teaching doesn't always "take," and kids tend to reflect the prejudices of their parents. Chances are, your group members will mouth the principles of equality, but may harbor fears and resentments.

If there has been a racial incident in your community, it may give your group members an opportunity to examine themselves, and to examine Scripture, to see how deep this "equality thing" goes.

Crisis #4: Racial Incident

Specific Aims

• To help group members recognize that God is "color blind"—He makes no distinction among people based on race; to help them understand that, because God loves all races equally, so should we who claim to be His children; and to help them support and encourage people who are picked on because of their race.

Scriptural Support

- Genesis 1:27; 9:24, 25; 11:8, 9
- Joshua 23:12, 13
- Luke 10:30-37
- Acts 17:26
- Romans 3:22, 23; 10:12, 13
- Galatians 3:28
- Ephesians 2:13-22

Special Preparation

- Bibles
- Copies of Student Sheet 4-A ("Case Studies")
- Copies of Student Sheet 4-B ("Biblical Rights and Wrongs")
- Pencils
- Newsprint and marker
- Tape

1 The Race Race

Map out an imaginary racetrack in your room. Show where the starting line is. Point out sharp turns, the "pit" area, grandstands, snack bars, etc. Explain that this racetrack stands for people's attitudes about race relations. Ask everyone to think about society's progress regarding race. Ask: **Regarding race, would you say most people in our society are at the starting line, running hard, sitting along the grandstands, in the pit area, etc.?** Have everyone choose a spot on the race course that indicates his or her opinion. Then ask volunteers to explain why they chose the spots they did.

Then ask group members to stand at a spot on the racetrack that best describes where most of the kids in their school are regarding race relations. Ask volunteers to explain why they chose the spots they did.

Then ask group members to choose a spot on the racetrack that best describes your church's attitudes about people of other races.

Finally, ask group members to select a spot that best shows where they would like to be regarding race relations.

Announce that you will be discussing racial issues, in light of the recent incident. [If there is not a specific incident prompting this session, you may want to rephrase the questions to be more general.]

Ask: **What happened?**

Who was involved?

Why did it happen?

What were the motives of the people involved?

There may be different versions of what happened, of who started what. You don't need to resolve this; you're not a grand jury.

Ask: **How are people feeling as a result of this incident? How do you feel about it?** Jot down answers to these two questions on taped-together sheets of newsprint as kids suggest them.

2 Case Studies

Distribute copies of Student Sheet 4-A ("Case Studies"). Divide into three groups. Ask each group to focus on one of the cases, reading it over carefully and answering the questions.

After 8-10 minutes bring the whole group together. Have someone from each group read the case study aloud and share his or her group's answers. After each one, ask: **Do you know anyone like this? Have you ever felt like this?**

When you've reviewed all of the cases, wrap up this section by asking: **What are some of the root causes of racial prejudice? What do you think are some of the underlying attitudes?** (Lack of understanding; pride; insecurity; fear, etc.)

How does the Christian faith relate to those attitudes? (It should combat them. We should be humbly learning to understand each other, trusting God for security and showing His love.)

3 Twisting Verses

Distribute copies of Student Sheet 4-B ("Biblical Rights and Wrongs"). Say: **It's hard to believe, but some people have actually used Scripture passages to defend the mistreatment of other races. Let's take a look at some of these verses, see how to interpret them properly, and then examine some other Scripture passages that show us the truth of the matter.**

Read each of the following passages aloud and briefly explain the misinterpretation. Then challenge group members to interpret each passage properly.

• Genesis 9:24, 25—Ham had disgraced his father, Noah, resulting in a curse on Ham's son, Canaan. Some claim Ham's other descendants migrated south, inhabiting Africa and becoming the black race. They also claim that this curse applies to all blacks, indicating that they should serve whites.

But the curse applied to Canaan, whose descendants settled not in Africa, but Canaan (Palestine).

• Genesis 11:8, 9—When all races were one, some claim, they angered God by building the Babel tower. So God separated them. And so, some would say, "What God has put asunder, let no man join together." We have no right, they say, to undo God's punishment.

But a quick look at Acts 2 shows God Himself undoing at Pentecost the damage of Babel. The sin of Babel was not unity, but pride, the idea that people didn't need God.

• Joshua 23:12, 13—Frequently the Israelites were warned against mingling with those of other nations. Some say these commands apply to races as well.

God Himself broke that barrier in the New Testament by throwing the doors open to Gentiles (which most modern Christians are). Interestingly, even in the Old Testament, God gave commands to welcome foreigners and refugees. Israelites were to be wary about adopting foreign practices, but they were to show kindness to the people.

• Acts 17:26—Paul tells the Athenians that God, overseeing human history, has established the timelines and boundaries of each nation. Some quote this as another indication that God intends each race to stay put, and not to mingle.

But that is not Paul's intent, as the context shows. Paul is showing God's control over human history. It is God, he says, who determined when the Babylonian Empire would rise and fall, as well as the Persian, and Alexander's, etc.

Read the following passages and explain God's real attitude toward the various races.

• Genesis 1:27—We are all made in God's image, whatever our race.

• Romans 3:22, 23—We have all sinned, and are all offered redemption, whatever our race.

• Romans 10:12, 13—Any of us, whatever our race, can call on God through Christ and be saved.

• Galatians 3:28—Whatever our race, we who believe are one in Christ Jesus.

4 Break Down the Walls

Say something like: **Racial prejudice is nothing new. People have been prejudiced since Bible times. In fact, it seems that much of the New Testament is dealing with that very issue—racial prejudice—not between blacks and whites or Hispanics or Asians, but between Jews and Gentiles, or non-Jews.**

The Jews of Jesus' day were very proud of their heritage. But a number of them tended to look down on everyone else. That's why the Good Samaritan story was so shocking.

Review the story of the Good Samaritan with the group (Luke 10:30-37). See if the kids can remember it without looking it up.

Ask: **Who was the true "neighbor" to the Jewish man who needed help?** (The Samaritan.)

How would Jesus' Jewish listeners have responded to this? (Surprise, shock, anger, guilt.)

Point out that God's goodness crosses racial boundaries. In this story, the Samaritan was acting more like one of "God's chosen people" than the Jewish leaders were. He was willing to help a person who probably hated him.

Say: **As Christianity spread to the Gentiles, many Jews had a problem with that. The Gentiles brought with them a shady past, and a lot of questionable customs. Besides, they didn't know all the Jewish rituals. But God was welcoming them into the church. Let's read what Paul said about it in Ephesians 2.**

Have someone read aloud Ephesians 2:13-18.

Ask: **What picture does Paul present here?** (A wall that Jesus breaks down.)

How did Jesus bring about this unity? (By His death on the cross.)

Then say: **Jesus can do the same thing today.**

Draw the group's attention to the statements you listed earlier on the newsprint. Explain that these are statements that can build walls between races. Point out the statements that show sinful pride. Point out those that define specific fears. Point out expressions of hate.

Say: **If we really believe in a God who gave Himself up for us, then whatever walls our pride has put up can be smashed to bits. If Jesus humbled Himself, so must we. Jesus' death takes away fear, because any suffering we might go through is nothing compared to the joy of following Him. The cross also demolishes hatred, because it shows a way of love and fills us with the ability to love others. If we really understood the cross, racism would be history.**

Invite the group, on cue, to rip the newsprint (and the symbolic wall) down. Really get into this, tearing the paper into strips, and pulling every remnant from the wall.

Ask: **How do you feel, after tearing down the newsprint?**

How can God's love help us tear down walls of hatred, fear, and pride? (God can teach us to see people of other races as He does—as humans deserving a chance to know and worship God.)

Bring the group into a circle and ask group members to place their arms on each other's shoulders. Ask someone to read aloud Ephesians 2:19-22. Ask: **What's the picture here?** (The people of the church are a temple being built.)

Invite group members to close their eyes and picture the temple under construction. Say: **Imagine the timbers connecting with each other. Picture the stones stacking up. The parts of the building are different, but they all fit together. Just like the temple, our lives should fit together with people who are different from us, stretching toward the sky and glorifying God.**

Close in prayer, asking God for strength in dealing with racial differences at school and in the community, and thanking Him for the cross and the unifying effect it has.

Case Studies

Bob (A white teenager)

I'm not prejudiced. I'm realistic. I'm white, and I don't like most of the black people I've met. I know that's not too cool to say, but at least I'm honest.

I guess I've always been taught that you make your own way in this world. You work hard for what you get. No one's going to give you anything. My dad works hard at his job so my sister and I can go to college. And I'm working hard in school so I can get a good job myself.

But black people—OK, not all, but most of them—act like the world owes them something. They sit back and wait to get favors. And if they don't get them, they cry about how poor and oppressed they are. Come on! The whole slavery thing was over—what, a hundred years ago? Isn't it about time to stop complaining?

I probably wouldn't care so much except for my dad. He was counting on a big promotion at work. That would put us over the top on my college fund. But a black woman, far less qualified, got the job. It was some affirmative action thing. So now I'm looking at community colleges for a year or two, then a transfer, maybe. And all my hard work is going down the drain.

Like I said, I'm not prejudiced. Just realistic. And pretty angry.

Questions

1. What sort of thing might Bob do if he got angry enough?

2. Do you agree with anything Bob says?

3. What does Bob need to understand to get a fuller picture?

Sharon (A black teenager)

Orientals make me nervous. I see them in school and they always have a ton of books in their hands, and they always stick together, and they never go to parties or anything, and they're always studying. And then they talk really fast, until they see you coming, and then they stop and look guilty. It makes you wonder what they're plotting.

My parents say they're buying up property in our neighborhood. They've started a couple of shops already, and they own some of the apartment buildings. And it's like there are always new ones in town. Every time you look up, someone's cousin is moving in for a few days, or a few weeks—and before long the whole town will be Asian.

Down the street there was a family that got behind on their rent. I knew the girl from school. Well, her parents split up and her mom was trying to stay there with the kids, but she didn't have the money. And, I don't know, it was three months, four months, but the landlord—he was Japanese, I think—kicked them out. Right out on the street. They had to move in with relatives in the next county. And the next day—the very next day—an Asian family moved right in. I mean, the refrigerator was still defrosting. Do you believe it?

I just don't trust them.

Questions

1. How do you think Sharon's lack of trust affects the way she treats Asian people?

2. Does she have good reasons not to trust Asians?

3. What does Sharon need to understand to get a fuller picture?

Kim (A Korean teenager)

I would really like to fit in, but not if it means changing who I am. I am proud of my family. My parents worked hard to establish themselves here. They have taught me many good things. But I find that most of the other girls at school don't care about these things.

I see the popular girls in school, the white girls, and I admire them in many ways. They have power, I think. Boys like them. They have a lot of friends. Teachers even show them special favor sometimes. I'd like to be like that, too. I'd like to "hang out" with them.

But they are always so concerned about how they look. Nothing else matters to them. They will be listening to you one moment and, if they pass a mirror, forget it. They always talk about boys and clothes, and nothing else. If I became like them, I would have to throw away so many things.

I am talking about honor, and respect for one's elders, and wisdom, and things of the soul. Not that you have to be serious all the time. But those girls just seem so—well, so silly. I guess that's why I usually spend time with my Asian friends. We understand each other—down deep.

Questions

1. How would you describe Kim's attitude?

2. Do you agree with Kim's analysis of white girls?

3. What things does Kim need to understand to get a fuller picture?

Biblical Rights and Wrongs

Scripture	*Misinterpretation*	*Truth of the Matter*
Genesis 9:24, 25	Since Ham's descendants migrated to Africa, all blacks are cursed.	______________________ ______________________ ______________________
Genesis 11:8, 9	God doesn't want races to live or work together.	______________________ ______________________
Joshua 23:12, 13	God does not want His people mingling with those of other races.	______________________ ______________________ ______________________
Acts 17:26	God has determined where each race should live.	______________________ ______________________

Other Scriptures	*What They Tell Us*
Genesis 1:27	____ ____
Romans 3:22, 23	____ ____
Romans 10:12, 13	____ ____
Galatians 3:28	____ ____

Session 5

When adults wrangle over doctrines, or styles, or strategies, young people often suffer. Church tensions bring out the worst in Christians. And teens, powerless, watch it all happen.

Church fights can do incredible damage to young faith. Teenagers are often idealistic; they see things in absolutes; they prize loyalty and love. When they see their elders being disloyal and unloving, they're tempted to chuck the whole thing. Goodbye, church. Goodbye, Christ.

Chances are, if your church is going through tension, you're in the middle of it—or at least strongly affected by the outcome. It would be easy to play your own politics, to save your own skin. But watch out for the kids. They'll pick up your attitudes. Before you teach this session, examine your own feelings, and offer them to Christ for cleansing.

Crisis #5: Church Split

Specific Aims

• To help group members hold onto Christ even when Christians fail them; to encourage them to maintain regular fellowship with believers, despite circumstances; and to affirm God's great plans for the church, even when it is wracked with discord.

Scriptural Support

• Acts 6:1-4; 15:1-6, 12, 22, 30-41
• I Corinthians 3:3-7
• Galatians 2:11-16
• Ephesians 4:15
• II Timothy 4:11
• I Peter 3:8, 9

Special Preparation

• Bibles
• Two copies of Student Sheet 5-A ("Motions and Emotions") for each group member
• Copies of Student Sheet 5-B ("Bible Brawls")
• Pencils
• Chalkboard and chalk or newsprint and markers
• Eyepatch (optional)

1 Ground Rules and a Strategy

Optional Opener—Have kids compete (juggling, drawing, etc.) with one eyepatch on and one hand behind the back. Afterward, discuss the difficulty of doing anything with only half the "body."

If your church is currently facing problems, announce that you are going to be talking about the problems the church is facing. If your church isn't currently facing a major problem, say something like: **We all know that the church is made up of people. Because of that, it's far from perfect. During this session, we're going to take a close look at problems that some churches, and perhaps eventually our church will face. But first we need to set up two ground rules and one strategy.** Write this on the board, if you like.

Ground Rule #1: People should be *honest*.

Ground Rule #2: People should be *loving*.

Explain that the Bible has a great phrase in Ephesians 4:15—"speaking the truth in love"—that explains how we grow, individually and as a group. This involves being honest about feelings, without trying to hurt anyone.

Explain that a strategy to help us "speak the truth in love" is using "I" statements. Say: **An "I" statement is a statement you make about yourself—what you think, how you feel. A "you" statement is what you say about someone else. Instead of saying, "You're ruining this church!"—that's a "you" statement—you might say, "I disagree with what you're doing," or, "I think that what you're doing will not be good for the church," or even, "I'm afraid about what will result from your actions."**

As the session proceeds, feel free to rephrase any of the group members' comments into "I" statements, if you feel it will help.

2 Third-Party Perspective

It's often easier to talk about conflict from an objective, "third-party" perspective. To help your kids begin to consider the issue of church splits, work through the following case study (based on a true story).

Read the following to the group:

A church was growing with its new minister. There had been struggles with former ministers, but things seemed to be going well under new leadership.

Then, Russ and Carol Engles joined the church. The Engles were a young, professional couple looking for a church home that would accept them and their two-year-old son, Aaron. They had been rejected by two other churches in town.

The issue was Aaron. He was adopted and was an AIDS victim. He'd had AIDS since birth.

When members of the congregation found out that Russ and Carol wanted to attend their church—and place Aaron in the nursery—they reacted with fear, anger, and hostility. Many threatened to leave the church if the child was allowed to attend the church nursery. Others, angry at that attitude, threatened to

leave the church if the child was *not* allowed in the nursery.

The minister didn't know what to do.

Finally, a church board meeting was called to decide how to deal with the situation.

Before continuing with this exercise, point out to your group members that AIDS is not easily transferred from one person to another. The disease is almost always caught through sexual activity, blood transfusions, intravenous drug use, or being born of a woman who has AIDS. A child is more likely to die on the car ride to church than to die of AIDS from being in the same nursery as an AIDS victim.

Distribute copies of Student Sheet 5-A ("Motions and Emotions"). Tell the group that you're going to discuss the issues that divide the church in this case. The goal is to understand where both sides are coming from.

Ask the kids to write down in the left column any of the charges or arguments they think the different factions might use. Give group members several minutes to list as many as they can.

Then ask volunteers to share one or two of their statements. After hearing each argument, ask how the other side might respond to that statement. Field several responses and let the kids choose one and jot it on the right side of the paper.

Move down the sheet to the "Emotions" section. Ask group members to circle any of the statements that express how they would feel if they were in that church. Have them put a star next to the one they would feel most strongly. After a minute or two, invite group members to talk about their responses.

Ask the group to examine the last part of the sheet. Say: **If there's one person in the church you could sit down and say something to about this issue, who would it be?** Ask volunteers what they would say to this person. Ask the group to suggest how that person might answer the question.

3 Getting Emotional about Motions

Ask group members to think about the issue that is currently threatening to split your church. If there is no pertinent issue, ask them to think about an issue that might split your church. Distribute new copies of Student Sheet 5-A ("Motions and Emotions"). Ask the group to jot down statements that people might say about the current situation.

Have volunteers read statements they've listed. Invite others to suggest how people who held the opposite view might respond.

Move on to the "Emotions" section. Instruct group members to circle the statements that describe their feelings. Invite them to place a star beside any statements about which they feel very strongly.

Ask volunteers to share their answers to the last two statements on the worksheet. Encourage others to suggest how people might respond to their statements.

4 Bible Brawls

Distribute copies of Student Sheet 5-B ("Bible Brawls"). Say: **Church fights are nothing new. Even in the Bible, Christians had major disagreements—including people like Paul, Peter, and Barnabas. This doesn't mean it's OK to fight with each other. It does mean it's not the end of the world. God's church continues to grow in spite of our problems.**

Break into five groups, assigning each group one of the Scripture passages on the sheet (or assign passages to individuals). Give the groups several minutes to read the passages and answer the questions. Then bring them together and have each group report.

Most of the answers are evident from the text. But zero in on Question #6. Across the board (with the possible exception of Corinth), the ultimate result was good. The Gospel went forth, the church became stronger, truth was clarified. Again, that doesn't mean that the conflicts were good. It just means that while people mess up, God can fix things.

5 Harmony

Have the group turn to I Peter 3:8, 9. Explain that this is one of many passages that tell us how to live with each other as Christians. Ask a group member to read it aloud. Then go back through it, listing the main ideas on the board and talking about them.

Live in harmony—Harmony occurs when different notes blend together. It's not unison. Harmony implies that people don't have to agree on everything. They just have to stay in tune.

Be sympathetic—This means feeling the feelings of the other people. Think about the people on the other side of your church conflict. How are they feeling right now?

Love as brothers—Brothers and sisters don't always get along with each other. They get into fights. But they also have deep love for each other.

Compassionate—Or "merciful." The idea is that you give the other person the benefit of the doubt. It's not always so important who's right and wrong.

Humble—Consider the other person's needs before yours.

Do not repay—Paybacks keep the vicious cycle going. Blessing stops it short. We are "called" to bless even those who persecute us. That's what Jesus did.

Ask: **How could you "bless" someone in this church who has been doing you wrong?** Challenge group members to come up with a specific action they could do in the next week to accomplish this. Have them write it on the back of the student sheet.

When all have had time to do this, close in prayer, asking God for strength to deal with divisions in a way that honors Him. Read I Peter 3:8, 9 again as a closing prayer.

MOTIONS AND EMOTIONS

WHAT ONE SIDE SAYS

1.

2.

3.

HOW THE OTHER SIDE WOULD RESPOND

1.

2.

3.

EMOTIONS
Circle any statements that express how church tensions make you feel.

1. I am so angry I want to punch somebody.

2. How can Christians be so unloving?

3. This stuff makes me dread coming to church.

4. If this is what Christians are like, I'm not sure I want to be one.

5. I am very disappointed with some people in this church.

6. I trust that God will make everything turn out all right.

7. Who's right and who's wrong? I am so confused, I don't know who to listen to anymore.

8. I wish I could do something to make everything better, but no one would listen to me.

9. No one cares what happens to the young people in all this.

The one person I'd like to sit down with and say something to is: ____________________
____

This is what I'd like to say: ____________________________________
____

BIBLE BRAWLS

Answer the questions for the Scripture passage you've been assigned.

SCRIPTURE

Group A—Acts 6:1-4
Group B—Acts 15:1-6, 12, 22, 30-35
Group C—Acts 15:36-41 (see also II Timothy 4:11)
Group D—I Corinthians 3:3-7
Group E—Galatians 2:11-16

QUESTIONS

1. What was the reason for the disagreement?

2. Which "side" do you think was right?

3. How would the other side explain its position (in 50 words or less)?

4. How do you think the people involved in this conflict felt?

5. How was it resolved?

6. What were the ultimate results of the controversy? (You may need to look at surrounding verses.)

Session 6

Unless you were vacationing on another planet in the late 1980s, you felt the tremors of the scandals involving several major Christian ministers. These events were disappointing, embarrassing, maddening, and saddening. Some people's faith was shaken. But the news also gave some Christians an opportunity to talk openly with non-Christians about the true nature of our faith.

Scandal is nothing new in the Christian church. Since the first century, the world has lured Christian leaders toward destruction. Some of the leaders who have been involved in scandals may have been rascals who used the church to gain power or wealth. But others are well-meaning folks who just fall under the pressure of temptation. And that pressure grows greater at higher altitudes.

Kids need to know that leaders are forgiven sinners, just as all Christians are. When a leader falls, whether far away or in your own church, young people need help to avoid cracks in the foundations of their faith.

Crisis #6: Scandal Involving a Christian Leader

Specific Aims

• To help group members understand the danger of placing our faith in a human being instead of in God; and to help them see the need for forgiveness for the fallen leader.

Scriptural Support

• Psalm 51:10-17
• Mark 14:66-72; 16:7
• John 8:1-11
• Romans 7:14, 15
• I Corinthians 3:5-9
• II Corinthians 4:7
• Galatians 6:1
• Philippians 1:14-18
• II Timothy 4:10
• Titus 1:7-9
• Revelation 2:2-5

Special Preparation

• Bibles
• Copies of Student Sheet 6-A ("How Do I Feel?")
• Copies of Student Sheet 6-B ("Scripture Search")
• Pencils
• Copies of a newspaper article with some words blacked out

1 Dangerous Misinformation

[NOTE: In most scandal situations, misinformation abounds. People know parts of the story, and they imagine the rest. It's important to help your group members weed out the untruths without violating the right to privacy of individuals. Present the facts of the case, as far as you know them, to the group. If you do not know certain details, say so. Throughout the session, strive to keep the discussion gossip-free. If some facts are disputed, acknowledge this. Try to be fair to all involved.]

To demonstrate the results of misinformation or incomplete information, open the session with a game. Distribute pencils and copies of a newspaper article in which you've blacked out crucial words. Have kids write their "complete" versions of the article based on guesswork. When everyone is finished, read the original article.

2 How Do I Feel?

If there is a leadership scandal in your church, your group members probably are awash with feelings of concern, anger, disappointment, etc. You need to get those feelilngs out into the open. Distribute copies of Student Sheet 6-A ("How Do I Feel?"). Instruct group members *not* to write their names on the sheets. Give them a few minutes to fill out the sheets. Explain to your group members that they should avoid judging the way individuals feel.

After everyone has had time to fill out the sheet, go through it, asking volunteers to share their answers. Don't force anything. Some group members may be shy about opening up their feelings.

Collect all of the worksheets. You may want to refer to them later as you evaluate this session and the impact of scandals on your youth group.

3 Scripture Search

Say: **You might think that the Bible says only good things about God's people, and sweeps the bad stuff under the rug. But no, the Bible is very honest about problems that occur. So, when our minds and hearts are full of tough questions, we can usually find answers in God's Word.**

Divide your group into five teams (or give assignments to individuals). Give each team or person a copy of Student Sheet 6-B ("Scripture Search"). Assign one of the questions to each team. After the teams have had a chance to answer their questions, ask them to share their answers with the entire group.

Use the following information to supplement your discussion of the passages.

Question #1—Paul was in jail, and some of his enemies were taking the opportunity to become famous teachers themselves. The passage shows that the Gospel is greater than the messenger. Even if Christ is preached for wrong reasons, He is still preached. The Gospel is still true. And the teaching still helps people.

Question #2—The Romans passage is a classic description of the struggle we all face. We still operate according to our physical desires, even though God has awakened the spiritual life in us. II Timothy 4:10 gives a brief look at Demas, who was apparently a coworker of Paul's, but left because he loved the world too much. That also can happen to us. Point out that in Revelation 2:2-5, the church seemed to be very busy doing good things, but had "forsaken its first love." When we stop doing things with the motive of love—for God and for others—all sorts of problems can creep in.

Question #3—John 8:1-11 should keep us all from judging others too hastily. All of us have sinned, so we mustn't "throw stones." Galatians 6:1 injects a note of caution. "Those who are spiritual" should restore the person "gently" and be careful about their own temptations. We should forgive, but keep seeking to obey God completely.

Question #4—These passages point out that God has strict standards for church leaders, but when a person truly repents, restoration is possible. Sin always creates damage, and the person will often bear the weight of this, but God's mercy is great toward those who ask forgiveness.

Question #5—We must not worship people, even great ministers. They are just servants of God, as we are. They—and we—are "jars of clay." Even when they shatter, God's purposes go forward.

4 Sarah and Rich

Have a group member read each of the following case studies, or read them aloud yourself.

Sarah

I became a Christian while watching Christine Lazar. She has a TV program on some cable channel, and every week she would teach the Bible. I discovered her by accident one day, and her words made sense to me like nothing else ever did. I sent in for her Bible study materials and read them. I felt so close to God as I heard her talk about Him. It seemed like she had all the answers to life every time she opened that Bible.

I even sent some of my money to support her work. She kept asking for money, so I kept sending it in.

So I was pretty upset when I read the news in the paper. Christine Lazar had been accused of lying. As the story came out, I learned that she had several large homes, a fleet of fancy cars, a plane, and a yacht. That's where all my money went. She never sent a penny to those earthquake victims in South America that she always talked about. It was all a trick.

I thought of all those great things she said about God. I guess she was just fooling everybody. She sure fooled me. I haven't read my Bible for awhile. I mean, what's the point?

Ask: **Do you understand how this person feels?**

How would you respond to this person's feelings?

Rich

I am steaming mad right now and I don't know what to do about it. I just learned that one of the elders in the church has been having an affair for the last five years with a woman in the church. How could he do such a thing? He has a great wife and two great kids, and yet he had to go off and fool around like that. It doesn't make sense.

I think back to a time when I had some serious questions. I was dating this girl from school at the time, a non-Christian, and we were just about to get sexually involved. I was really struggling with it all, so I went to this elder to talk about it. And he was so cool. He just explained to me why my relationship with Jesus was more important than anything else, and I wouldn't want to do anything to mess that up. It was hard, but I broke up with that girl, because the relationship just wasn't good for me. And that elder helped me out a lot with that. He helped me see straight.

But now I find out that, at the same time, he was having an affair. How could he tell me to be holy, when he was being so unholy? I mean, why did I have to break up with this girl, when he kept seeing this other woman? It's just not fair.

If I ever see him again, I think I'll punch him out. Really. And they tell me he wants to apologize to the whole church, to put it all behind him. He's going to take a leave of absence and then come back to be an elder again. Not if I can help it!

Ask: **Do you understand how this guy feels?**

What would you say to him?

5 The Ministerial Review Board (optional)

If your group is mature enough, and if you think group members need help to forgive the leader who has fallen, try the following simulation.

Recruit three volunteers. One person will play the role of "Reverend Smythe." He has been accused of having an affair. He admits to having the affair, but has asked forgiveness from all involved.

The other two volunteers will play the roles of "representatives." The first representative will try to convince the board (the rest of your group) that Reverend Smythe should receive the harshest punishment the board can give. The second representative should push for a lesser penalty.

Introduce the situation and call on Reverend Smythe to explain his current stand. Then ask the two representatives to make their appeals to the board.

Give members of the board a chance to ask questions of the three, and to make suggestions about what the final response of the board will be. Have them vote for the best suggestion.

Then ask: **How hard was it to come up with a decision?**

Do you think your final decision was fair?

Would you offer a similar decision for our current situation (if your church is currently facing a scandal)?

6 Prayer Time

Ask your group members to suggest ideas of what to pray for concerning the subject of this session. (Suggestions might include the persons involved in the scandal, the family or others close to the scandal, the faith of everyone who might be disillusioned by this, and the church as a whole.) You might want to make a list of the requests on the board as they are named. Pray for all the requests.

How Do I Feel?

Place an X on each line below to show how you feel right now.

This is how I feel.	***This is not how I feel.***	
___	___	1. I am shocked.
___	___	2. I feel betrayed.
___	___	3. I am concerned for this person's relationship with God.
___	___	4. I am concerned for this person's family.
___	___	5. I am angry.
___	___	6. I wonder if this person really believed the things he (or she) said about God.
___	___	7. I forgive this person.
___	___	8. I think we should all just forget the whole thing.
___	___	9. I feel tempted to disobey God, too. If this person can do it, why can't I?
___	___	10. This whole thing is making me question my own beliefs about God.

If I could sit down and talk with this person right now, I would say something like this:

____

____

____

Scripture Search

Some Questions You May Have That the Bible Can Answer

1. Does this scandal mean that everything this person taught is untrue? (Philippians 1:14-18)

2. How can a scandal like this happen to a Christian? (Romans 7:14, 15; II Timothy 4:10; Revelation 2:2-5)

3. How should we respond to this person? (John 8:1-11; Galatians 6:1)

4. Can such a person ever be restored to a leadership position? If so, under what terms? (Psalm 51:10-17; Mark 14:66-72; 16:7; Titus 1:7-9)

5. What should our attitude be toward our church leaders? (I Corinthians 3:5-9; II Corinthians 4:7)

Session 7

This is a tricky issue. Handle it with care. The young couple's life will be changed. The two may be making crucial decisions right now. More than ever, they need the help of their Christian friends.

How should your group respond? Not by placing blame, but by learning to deal with a tough situation. Condemnation, rejection, and criticism might be natural responses for many in your group, but healing will take place only as people accept and welcome the girl and boy. You can help to uphold a biblical standard for sex—and a biblical standard for compassion.

Crisis #7: Pregnant Teen

Specific Aim

• To help group members understand the importance of reaching out to unwed mothers and fathers in a compassionate, nonjudgmental manner; and to help them reassess their own sexual behavior.

Scriptural Support

- Psalm 103:8-14
- Lamentations 3:22-24
- Hosea 14:1, 2, 4, 9
- John 3:19-21; 8:3-11
- Romans 6:19-23
- Ephesians 2:4-10
- James 1:13-15

Special Preparation

- Bibles
- Copies of Student Sheet 7-A ("Attitudes")
- Copies of Student Sheet 7-B ("Love and Death")
- Pencils
- A "thinking of you" card

1 Examine-a-Case

If a member of your group (or a friend of your group) has recently become pregnant, begin by announcing the situation as frankly as you can (if you have the permission of the pregnant girl). Give whatever information is necessary, but don't reveal anything that is not pertinent. (If you feel uncomfortable airing such "dirty laundry" before the whole group, you might want to hold a special session sometime for close friends of the couple and use this material then.)

If your group is not currently facing a pregnancy situation, use the following case study to help group members begin thinking about the subject.

Karen got pregnant. She didn't plan it. She didn't want to be pregnant. But she did, and now she must face the consequences.

Karen was active in your group. So was Jeff, her boyfriend. Everyone liked them. But now, people are beginning to talk. Some are calling Karen names. Some are spreading rumors.

Neither Karen nor Jeff has returned to the youth group since Karen became pregnant. Both are probably too embarrassed.

So, what do you do?

Encourage several volunteers to respond.

2 Attitudes

Distribute copies of Student Sheet 7-A ("Attitudes"). Explain that these six statements reflect attitudes that people might have about teenage pregnancy. In the space before each statement, the group members should circle "Yes," "No," or "Sort Of," indicating whether or not they agree with the statement. They may also write comments after the statements. Announce that you will not collect the papers, but you will discuss them.

After group members have responded, ask them to place an "X" by those statements that adults in your church would tend to agree with and a check mark by those statements that kids in their school might agree with.

Give group members about five minutes to work on the sheets; then begin the discussion. Go through the statements one by one, asking volunteers how they responded. Use the following information to supplement your discussion.

1. Birth control might have prevented pregnancy (though it doesn't always work), but that's not the extent of their problem. Unmarried people should not have sex to begin with.

2. Abortion is not an easy way out for anyone involved. [Avoid getting into a full-scale discussion of abortion right now. Just help your group members understand that abortion raises a lot of new problems for the couple, including the right of the unborn baby to live.]

3. Marriage does not make premarital sex all right. And premarital sex—or even a pregnancy—is no reason to force a marriage. Many bad marriages result from such reasoning. Don't let one mistake cause another. Marriage *might* be a

good choice at this point, if the young people are ready for it and spiritually compatible; but it's not the only choice.

4. These kids need the love of their friends more than ever. And we all need to experience sharing love with someone in need.

5. Pregnancy is a result of sex, not God's punishment. God often allows us to reap the natural results of our sinful behavior. Thinking of this as punishment could also affect the way we view the baby—who deserves the same start in life that we all do.

6. The problem is that they sinned, and they're throwing a lot of people's lives into a spin cycle. Things may turn out all right, by God's mercy, but not unless they deal with the issue of sin.

Ask: **In what ways do you think adults in our church might disagree with your responses?**

How do you think other kids in your school might feel about this situation?

Why are there such differing opinions?

3 Sin and Its Consequences

Distribute copies of Student Sheet 7-B ("Love and Death"). Say: **Let's look at the results of sin. There are many Bible verses that indicate that premarital sex is sinful. The question we want to focus on now is: What happens to us when we sin?**

Ask a volunteer to read aloud each of these passages for "Theme One" and then discuss them one at a time as a group. Use the following information to supplement your discussion.

- James 1:13-15—Desire leads to sin, which leads to death. Sin grows as it controls more and more of a person, and removes that person from God. It distracts, it blinds. The "death" is primarily a separation from God, who is the source of all life.
- Romans 6:19-23—Sin controls a person, enslaves a person. The person can no longer make free choices. The "wages of sin" are death; not that God immediately strikes down the one who sins, but He offers forgiveness through Christ so that we can avoid eternal death.
- John 3:19-21—Jesus is the light, the full radiance of God's truth and holiness. Evildoers stay away from the light because it reveals their shortcomings. As Adam and Eve hid from God in the garden, so we often try to cover up our sin by staying away from God. Christians who are wrapped up in sin, who desperately need God's forgiveness, often stop coming to church or talking with Christian friends, because they are now uncomfortable in the "light." This is part of the process by which sin grows within us and enslaves us.

In responding to the statement, point out that God does forgive, but each time we sin, we step away from Him. Each sin makes it easier to sin again. Eventually we may reach a point where we don't want to come back for God's forgiveness anymore. Sin can enslave us.

4 God's New Mercy

Now focus on "Theme Two" of Student Sheet 7-B. As before, go through the passages one by one. Use the following information to supplement your discussion of the passages.

• Lamentations 3:22-24—God's love preserves us. He is "faithful" to us. "New every morning" indicates that He always takes us from the point where we are. Each day is a new day. We can return to Him at any moment and start anew.

• Ephesians 2:4-10—God made us alive when we were dead in sin. We can do nothing to earn His favor. Good works are the *result* of coming to life, not the cause.

• Psalm 103:8-14—God removes our sins as far as the east is from the west (as far as possible). In His compassion, He realizes that we can't obey Him perfectly apart from His Spirit.

• Hosea 14:1, 2, 4, 9—God will "heal our waywardness" when we return to Him. He can help us obey Him. The rebellious stumble because they have determined not to cry out to God for help.

In responding to the statement at the bottom of the page, point out that God always wants us back. All of us have sinned, and God wants to forgive us for everything. All we have to do is turn to Him. He will do the rest.

5 So What?

Say something like: **We've learned two important things today about sin and forgiveness. Sin has its price, which is why God doesn't want us to do it; and, we can be forgiven for our sins.**

What does all this have to do with pregnancy? Well, these are the things we have to keep in mind as we deal with this couple. On the one hand, we can't ignore that there was sin involved. But that should make us take a hard look at our own lives and see where we might be straying from God.

We know that God forgives us for our sins, and that He wants to forgive this couple. He also wants to lead them through the difficult choices that lie ahead.

Ask someone to read John 8:3-11 aloud. Ask: **What was Jesus' response to a woman who was guilty of having sex outside of marriage?** (He forgave her.)

What did He say to the Pharisees who brought her to Him? (He indirectly pointed out their guilt.)

Did Jesus give the woman permission to keep sinning? (No. He accepted her, forgave her, and told her not to go on living in sin.)

In what ways can we show God's love and forgiveness for this couple? What can we do, even in the next week or two, to help them?

Discuss group members' ideas.

Pass around a "thinking of you" card. Ask each person in the group who wants to, to write a sincere note and sign the card. During the next week, send (or better yet, personally deliver) the card.

In closing, pray that God would show His compassion to the couple, and guide them in the weeks ahead. Ask Him to help each person deal honestly with this issue. Thank Him for His forgiveness.

Attitudes

Circle "Yes," "No," or "Sort Of" to indicate whether you agree or disagree with each of the following statements. You may want to jot some thoughts down in the space under each statement.

Yes No Sort Of 1. They were just dumb. They should have used birth control. That was their main mistake.

Yes No Sort Of 2. The best thing to do now is to get an abortion. They obviously can't raise a child at their age.

Yes No Sort Of 3. They have to get married now, since they were already having sex. That will make everything all right.

Yes No Sort Of 4. They are obviously not walking with God. Other Christians should stay away from them, so they don't get tempted themselves.

Yes No Sort Of 5. This pregnancy is God's punishment for having premarital sex.

Yes No Sort Of 6. What's the problem? They'll just grow up a bit faster than they expected to. The experience of parenthood will be good for them.

Examine the statements again. Place an "X" beside each statement that you think most of the adults in your church would agree with. Place a check mark beside each statement that you feel kids in your school would agree with.

Love and Death

Theme One: Sin has deadly results.

Read James 1:13-15.
1. How does this passage describe the process of sin?

2. How does sin "grow"?

3. What do you think "death" means in this passage?

Read Romans 6:19-23.
1. What does it mean to be a "slave" to sin?

2. What are the "wages of sin"?

3. What do you think "death" means in this passage?

Read John 3:19-21.
1. What is the "light"?

2. How do evildoers respond to the light?

3. Have you ever experienced this sort of thing in your own life?

In light of these passages, how would you respond to the Christian who says, "Hey, I can have sex as much as I like and still be a good Christian. God is love. If what I'm doing is wrong, He'll forgive me. It really doesn't matter. As long as I'm careful about it, protect myself from pregnancy and diseases, and don't hurt anybody, there's no problem."

Theme Two: God cares.

Read Lamentations 3:22-24.
1. From the previous passages we've looked at, you get the idea that sin should drag us all into slavery. According to Lamentations, what keeps us from being "consumed"?

2. Why is it important that the Lord's compassion is "new every morning"?

Read Ephesians 2:4-10.
1. When did God make us "alive with Christ"? (See verse 5.)

2. Is our salvation dependent on our goodness?

3. What part do "good works" have in our lives?

Read Psalm 103:8-14.
1. What does God do with our sins?

2. Why is it important that God knows "we are dust"?

Read Hosea 14:1, 2, 4, 9.
1. What does God promise to do for those who return to Him?

2. Who "stumbles" in God's ways? (See verse 9.)

In light of these passages, how would you respond to the person who says, "I've gone too far. I've been sleeping around and I've gotten into a lot of bad stuff. I used to be a nice Christian kid, but I lost all of that. There's no way God would want me back. I'm too much of a mess."

Session 8

Over 1.25 million divorces occur each year in the United States. That's about 150 *per hour.* About 70% of these divorces involve parents with children under 18 years of age. So, about twice a minute in this country, a kid sees his or her family broken apart. Another sobering figure: A 1980 study found only 5% of children affected by divorce being counseled or helped by a church or minister (*Children of Divorce,* Jim and Barbara Dycus [David C. Cook, 1987]).

It would be nice to think this doesn't happen in the church. You know better. Christian marriages break up, too. And sometimes the church's reaction only makes things worse—especially for the kids. It's your mission to make things better—not all better, but a little better.

Crisis #8: Divorce

Specific Aims

• To help kids whose parents haven't divorced get an idea of how devastating divorce is so they can empathize with others; to give kids whose parents have divorced an opportunity to share their feelings about it; and to help kids understand that their relationship with God will *never* end.

Scriptural Support

- Genesis 21:14-20
- James 1:27

Special Preparation

- Bibles
- Copies of Student Sheet 8-A ("How Does It Feel?")
- Copies of Student Sheet 8-B ("The Aftershocks of Divorce")
- Pencils

1 A Moving Experience

As you begin this session, you should be aware of your church's position on divorce, since that question may be raised. [NOTE: Be sensitive to any kids whose parents have just split up. Such a group session might be hard for them to take. You might want to consult with them beforehand.]

Ask group members to stand up and to start walking around the room. They may greet their friends as they pass them, but they should keep moving. When you say **Stop**, they should pair up quickly with the person closest to them and stand facing each other. (If there's an odd number, you'll have to join the game yourself.) When they have done this, explain that they should finish this sentence to their partner: "I appreciate you because . . ." Give them no more than 20 seconds before telling them to get moving again, walking around the room.

As they walk, ask them to identify something negative about themselves—something they've done wrong at some point, or some personality flaw. Explain that you'll be asking them to tell this to someone else, so it can't be too personal. Say **Stop** a second time, and have them pair up, as before. This time, ask each one to tell the other person about this negative thing. In response, the other person should say, "I appreciate you anyway."

Give them no more than 30 seconds and get them moving again. Have them think about a time in their lives when they really needed to be appreciated, when they felt sad or lonely or down on themselves. Say **Stop** one more time and have them pair up again. Have them share this moment of need with each other.

Give them about a minute and then have them return to their seats. You might want to ask them how they felt about the game, which was the hardest thing to say, etc.

2 Why We're Here

Explain that you're going to be talking about divorce and the needs that arise when there is a divorce in your family. One of the greatest needs is merely to be appreciated, which is one reason for the silly game you've just played.

Encourage the kids to talk frankly about their feelings, but to be respectful to the people involved if they mention actual cases. Explain that this session will not discuss the biblical teaching on divorce—the right or wrong of specific situations. Instead, you will be talking about how to deal with divorce if it happens in your own family, and how to support other kids from broken homes.

3 How Does It Feel?

Hand out Student Sheet 8-A ("How Does It Feel?"). Explain that there are a lot of different feelings kids go through when their parents divorce. Some possible feelings are listed on the student sheet. Kids with divorced parents should choose the three words or phrases that best describe the way they felt in the year or so after their parents' divorce. The others should choose the three words or phrases that best describe the way they think kids would be affected by their parents' divorce. In the lines beneath the words, they all should write a sentence or two explaining why they felt (or why someone would feel) that way.

Give them about five minutes to work on the student sheet; then talk about it. Ask volunteers to share the three feelings they chose and explain why they chose them. Ask if anyone was surprised by any answers.

Then say something like: **These are all very natural and normal ways to feel. But a lot of times, we have no idea why we feel the way we do. When we really think about the reasons, we realize some of these feelings don't make a lot of sense. We need to move on, to move through some of these feelings and really deal with the situation.**

Remind the group that feelings are not right or wrong. They just happen; we don't always choose to have them. But as we see the situation in a new way, we can change our feelings. It is not "wrong" to feel angry or guilty or depressed about your parents' divorce. It can be unhealthy, however, if you stay in this mood for a long time. Good friends can coax a person out of some unhealthy feelings by just listening, by reassuring, or by offering a friendly hug.

4 Facing Falsehoods

Hand out Student Sheet 8-B ("The Aftershocks of Divorce"). Divide into small groups. (If possible, try to disperse kids from broken homes among the groups.) Ask each group to go over the statements on the sheet and come up with a group response to each one. Give the groups seven or eight minutes, then bring them together to talk about it.

Use the following information to supplement your discussion of the sheet.

Tom

The divorce is not about the kids. It's about the couple. It is very rare that kids would cause a divorce, and it is nearly impossible for a kid to do something to undo a divorce. The guilt is unfounded.

Fred

First, it is likely that *the parents both love the kids, but feel they can't live together.* Second, it is possible that the parents really love the kids, but are caught up in *their own emotional turmoil.* We all make some decisions that hurt people we love. Third, *even if the parents fail to love the kids, that does not mean the kids don't have worth.* It means the parents are not thinking clearly. We are all valuable in God's eyes.

Louise

God loves people; He hates sin. God will forgive our sin, even divorce. Even if divorce is a selfish decision, it is not beyond God's forgiveness.

Greg

God is in control of our lives. The fact is, we don't control our own situations. At any moment, a car accident, an earthquake, or the Publisher's Clearing House Sweepstakes could drastically change our lives. We are all dependent on God each day. Yes, the security of the home may be shattered, but God will provide what is necessary.

Suzanne

Parents are human, too. But they're still parents. God requires obedience, even when that's difficult. In fact, divorced parents need more love and emotional support now than ever.

5 THE SCRIPTURE PICTURE

Ask a volunteer to read aloud James 1:27.

Ask: **How does James define true religion?** (Caring for widows and orphans; keeping oneself holy in an unholy world.)

Who are "widows and orphans"? If no one mentions it, point out that the obvious answer is that they are women and children whose husbands and fathers have died. But families involved in divorce often have similar needs, and widows and orphans are frequently set apart for special care in Scripture because they need it. Faithful believers must care for the physical and emotional needs of these broken families.

Ask: **Does the desire to keep ourselves from being "polluted" by the world have anything to do with our care for the victims of divorce?** If no one mentions it, point out that some Christians stay away from divorced people and their families because they're afraid they'll be "contaminated." But the Bible indicates we must get involved with people who are in need, and show love and care. We must also guard against the idea that divorce is nothing to worry about, that marriage is only a temporary thing. We should keep our standards for marriage even as we care for those in need.

Ask group members to turn to Genesis 21:14-20. As they do, explain that Scripture gives us few examples of divorced people. One is the woman at the well, who had been married five times—and still Jesus offered her living water. Another example is Hagar.

The kids will need this background before they read:

God promised to give Abraham a son. Since Abraham was getting old, he and Sarah decided he should father a child by her servant-woman, Hagar. Hagar gave birth to the boy Ishmael. But then God told Abraham that the promised child would be born to Sarah, his wife, and not to Hagar. And so Abraham, in a way, "divorced" Hagar, sending her and Ishmael away.

Ask: **How would you describe Hagar and Ishmael's attitude after being sent away?** (Very sad; rejected; depressed; maybe angry.)

Had God forgotten about Ishmael? What was He planning to do? (He was going to make Ishmael into "a great nation." This was a promise that the boy would live a long life and have many children.)

Say something like: **God says the same thing to kids from divorced families today. "I have not forgotten you. I have great plans for you." We all can help spread that message to the people who need it. We can be the ones who, like Hagar, bring the cold water to the kids who think they're dying alone in the desert. We can show them God's love.**

6 Touch Service

Divide the group into two smaller groups. Explain that this has been a tough session, and it's always good to receive a bit of affirmation. Ask the members of one group to bow their heads and close their eyes. Then, ask members of the second group to quietly stand up, walk over to the first group and touch people that they want to affirm. By placing a hand on a shoulder, or giving a small hug, they can say to that person, "You are important!" (Make sure that all group members get touched.)

After a minute or two, ask the people in the second group to return to their seats, bow their heads, and close their eyes. Give everyone in the first group a chance to affirm the second group by touch.

Then close in prayer, asking God to help each group member to care for others in need.

HOW DOES IT FEEL?

Choose three words or phrases from this list. If your parents are divorced, choose the three that best describe how you felt in the year or so after their divorce (or right now, if the divorce is recent). If your parents are not divorced, choose the three words or phrases that best describe how you think kids react to divorce. After you've made your choices, write a sentence or two explaining the reasons for your feelings.

Angry at parents

Physically sick

Guilty

Relieved

Worrying about the future

Determined to get parents back together

Pretending it didn't happen

Depressed

Mad at God

Hating yourself

Needing attention

Very close to one parent, against the other

Unable to love others

Unable to trust others, especially the opposite sex

Close to God

Judging others

Confused

Wanting to be alone

Finding it hard to focus attention

Not wanting to be alone

First Choice: ______________________________

Why? ______________________________

____

Second Choice: ______________________________

Why? ______________________________

____

Third Choice: ______________________________

Why? ______________________________

____

The Aftershocks of Divorce

The following statements have mistakes in them. In the space provided, write how you would respond to a friend who said this.

Tom

"It's my fault. If I were a better kid, my parents would still be together. If I were smarter, I could find a way to get them back together."

Fred

"If my parents really loved me, they'd stay together. Since they insist on splitting up, I must not be very important to them. I'm not worth much anyway."

Louise

"God hates people who divorce. My parents are doomed in God's eyes. They will never be able to have a close relationship with God or be active members of a church."

Greg

"My whole life is out of control. There's no telling what will happen. If my parents marry again, I could be out on the street. If we don't have enough money, I won't get to college, and then my life will be ruined."

Suzanne

"Parents always tell us how to do right, and then they mess up. Now I can't believe anything they say. How can they teach me, when they need teaching themselves?"

Session 9

You get a call in the middle of the night from a member of your group. "Help! I'm at the police station. I don't know what to do." Or, the parents call you a day or two later to talk about their son's arrest. Or, you hear about it through the kids' grapevine.

It can shake you. Crime often leads to more crime. The kid's life is going down the tubes, it seems, and you're saying, "What could I have done to save him?"

Maybe nothing. But you—and your youth group—can be a significant force in the delinquent teen's rehabilitation. That's what this session is about—not just debriefing the kids and helping them with the shock, but enlisting and equipping them to help bear the burdens of the kid in trouble.

Crisis #9: Arrest of a Friend

Specific Aim

• To help kids understand the encouragement they can provide to a friend in trouble, by being an instrument of God's forgiveness.

Scriptural Support

• Matthew 25:31-40
• Luke 15:11-32; 23:39-43
• Romans 15:1, 2, 7
• Ephesians 4:25-32
• Colossians 3:13

Special Preparation

• Bibles
• Copies of Student Sheet 9-A ("The Case of the Missing Son")
• Copies of Student Sheet 9-B ("Scripture Study")
• Pencils
• Chalkboard and chalk or newsprint and marker

1 Charting the Progression of Crime

If someone close to your group has been recently arrested, you may find it necessary to present the news to the group and update it as clearly as possible. When you do so, present just the facts. Steer the group away from sharing rumors or gossip that can only complicate the issue.

You may need to set some ground rules by saying something like: **As many of you know, "Bobby"** [or whoever] **has gotten into some serious trouble. We are going to talk frankly about his situation, because we want to help him. It doesn't do any good to overlook a problem like this. But we love "Bobby"—and God loves "Bobby." Everything we say here should be said with that in mind. We may not like the things "Bobby" has done, but we love him and want to support him.**

Draw on the board the following Crime Progression Chart (before the session, if possible), explaining that this is the way things often work for a kid who gets in trouble.

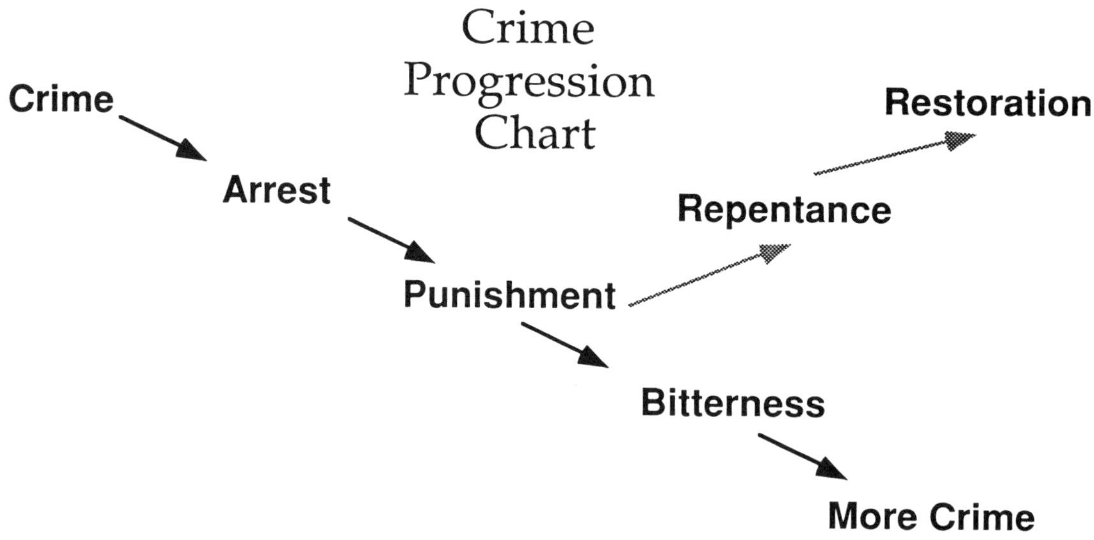

Explain the chart by saying something like: **A person gets involved with crime, for whatever reason—greed, drugs, pressure from friends, violence. If this continues, eventually there probably will be an arrest. There probably also will be punishment. Sometimes the punishment sobers the person up. The person repents—confesses to God and turns away from sin—and is restored to the church and society.**

Now, as "Bobby's" friends, what should we be trying to do? Well, we basically want to help him move through the progression. Repentance can occur at any time. We need to do all we can to steer him toward repentance and restoration.

2 THE CASE OF THE MISSING SON

Present a short drama. Explain that you're not trying to make light of a bad situation, but are trying to look at a familiar Bible story in a fresh way.

Distribute copies of Student Sheet 9-A ("The Case of the Missing Son") and assign roles. You may ask the cast to act the skit out fully, as on stage, or to perform it as a "radio play," with voices only.

After the skit is presented, talk about it. Remind the group that it is a retelling of the familiar prodigal son story from Luke 15 (summarize the parable, if needed). Ask these questions:

How did the son expect the father to treat him when he returned? (The Bible story makes clear that the son expected rejection, and was ready to plead for mercy.)

What was the father's attitude when the son returned? (He was overjoyed, ready to celebrate, ready to forgive all.)

Who was the villain in this story? What was this person's problem? (The older brother—or, in our story, the sister—was jealous and resentful, and did not join in the celebration.)

How does God respond when a wrongdoer comes back to Him? (As the father did, graciously, joyously.)

In what way might we be like the older brother/sister? How can we avoid this? (We often respond in judgment and self-righteousness. We should try to take the Father's point of view, longing for the person's repentance and rejoicing when it happens.)

3 SCRIPTURE STUDY

Hand out Student Sheet 9-B ("Scripture Study"). This is the worksheet for the Bible study that will follow. Write the following Scripture references on the board. Instruct each group member to choose two to study.

- Matthew 25:31-40
- Luke 23:39-43
- Romans 15:1, 2, 7
- Ephesians 4:25-32
- Colossians 3:13

Ask the group members to read the passages, and then answer the questions on the sheet. Explain that the questions may not always have obvious answers.

Give group members several minutes to work on the sheets. Then talk about group members' findings, using the following information to supplement your discussion.

Matthew 25:31-40—Christ identifies with people in need (including those in prison). We should serve these people as we would serve Christ.

Luke 23:39-43—Christ forgave a repentant thief on the cross. We should have the same attitude.

Romans 15:1, 2, 7—Christ forgives our sins. We should forgive others, and welcome them, even if their faith is weak.

Ephesians 4:25-32—God wants people to live righteously, but He has forgiven us of our sins; therefore, we must be forgiving toward each other.

Colossians 3:13—God has forgiven us so much, we must forgive and "put up with" each other.

4 So What?

Say something like: **We have been talking a lot about forgiveness. But sometimes we can get the idea that God doesn't really care if we sin. "Go ahead," we picture Him saying, "that's OK, I forgive you."**

But it is clear from the Ephesians passage and others that God hates sin. It hurts Him—especially when Christians do it. That's not the way it's supposed to be! But still it happens. And when we confess our sins, God forgives.

Make no mistake. If "Bobby" is truly guilty, we shouldn't make light of what he did. He sinned. He displeased God. But Jesus died for that sin, and we need to remind "Bobby" of that fact.

Refer to the chart you used earlier. Point out the tendency for sin to drag us down. Sinning makes it easier to sin a second time, and a third. Sin can produce bitterness, which leads to more sin, and so on. It's a downward spiral. It's a trap.

Say: **Our job as Christian friends is to open the doors of repentance at any point along the way. If we show the person a way out of this jam, he just might take it. If we show that repentance leads to a great new relationship with God, and the warm, accepting love of other Christians, we can make it much more appealing. On the other hand, if we respond with judgmental attitudes, we make it that much harder for the person to come back to God.**

Brainstorm together to discover specific ways of helping a person who has been arrested. List the suggestions on the board. You might encourage the kids to consult their copies of Student Sheet 9-B ("Scripture Study") for ideas. If you like, plan some group methods of ministering to a kid in trouble.

Close in prayer, asking God to give each group member a heart of forgiveness and acceptance, and to strengthen the arrested young person in his or her time of need.

THE CASE OF THE MISSING SON

CAST: Detective, Father, Leah, Casino Girl, Louie

DETECTIVE: It was a dark night. I got a distress call from a father—said his son was gone. I get calls like this all the time. The name's Marlowe, Fred Marlowe, Private Snoop. I guessed that this man had money to pay. He gave me an address in one of the swankier 'burbs. I went right over. He met me at the door.

FATHER: Thanks for coming. I'm concerned about my son, Louie. He's still a teenager and—well, he took off with his share of the inheritance.

DETECTIVE: Grand theft, huh?

FATHER: No, it was his money to take. I'm just worried about him.

DETECTIVE: So you suspect foul play? A kidnapping?

FATHER: No, he left on his own free will. I just don't want him to get into too much trouble.

DETECTIVE: So you want me to find him and bring him back?

FATHER: Only if he wants to come. But please, make sure he's all right.

DETECTIVE: *(to audience)* Dad got a phone call, so he asked his daughter, Leah, to show me to the door. I tried to make small talk. *(To LEAH)* I bet you're pretty worried about Louie, huh?

LEAH: Louie who?

DETECTIVE: *(to audience)* Just as I thought. Sibling rivalry. I checked with a pal in the credit bureau. Louie was leaving a paper trail from Las Vegas to Atlantic City. I flashed his picture around the casinos.

CASINO GIRL: Oh, yeah, I remember him. He was gambling like there was no tomorrow. Bought me these earrings, too. Sweet guy. But the next day he was gone.

DETECTIVE: Where?

CASINO GIRL: Florida, I think. He kept talking about Miami Vice.

DETECTIVE: I found him in the outskirts of Orlando, working for a bookie named Jimmy the Gypsy, taking bets over the phone. He was all alone in a dark, musty office.

LOUIE: Who are you?

DETECTIVE: Friend of your dad's.

LOUIE: Look, I don't have any money left, so just leave me alone.

DETECTIVE: How much do they pay you here, Louie?

LOUIE: Not enough.

DETECTIVE: My guess is that you welched on a few bets, and instead of breaking your legs, the Gypsy put you to work for him.

LOUIE: Yep.

DETECTIVE: I'd bet that your dad pays the paperboy more than you're getting.

LOUIE: But I couldn't go back. Not after losing all that money. He'd never take me back.

DETECTIVE: I wouldn't be so sure, kid. It's worth a try. *(To audience)* The kid made it back home and, wouldn't you know, his father met him at the curb.

FATHER: My son, you're back. It's so good to see you!

LOUIE: I'm sorry, Dad. Look, I don't deserve a thing. Just let me deliver papers to you or bring you your coffee. I'll set up a tent out back—

FATHER: Nonsense! You're my son! Leah, call the caterers. Order us a feast! We're going to party! *(FATHER and LOUIE exit.)*

DETECTIVE: *(To LEAH)* What's the matter, sweetheart? You look glum.

LEAH: He never threw me a party. The kid blows the family fortune and gets welcomed back like an astronaut. Where's the sense in that?

DETECTIVE: I don't know. Seems to me you've had it pretty easy, living off the old man's money. I wouldn't complain if I were you. To your dad, your brother was lost—died. He's just glad to have him back. *(To audience)* She went off in a huff. Dames! They're like that. But that's all for this case. There's a party going on!

Scripture Study

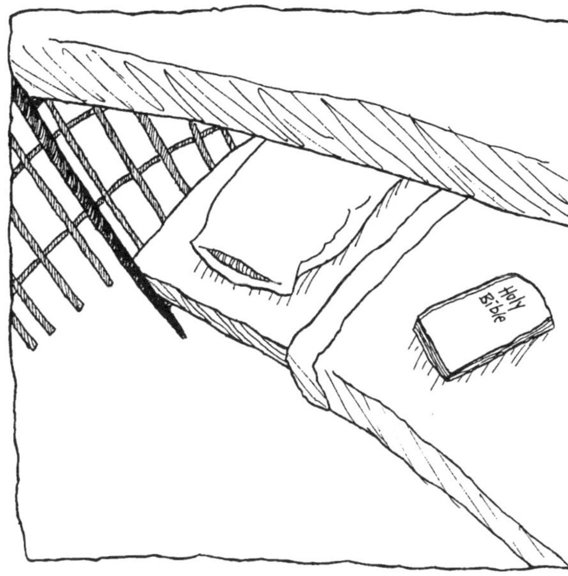

Study #1

Passage of Scripture studied: ____________________

1. What can I learn from this passage about God's attitude toward the person in trouble?

2. According to this passage, what should my attitude be toward the person in trouble?

3. What is one specific thing I can do as a result of reading this passage?

Study #2

Passage of Scripture studied: ______________________

1. What can I learn from this passage about God's attitude toward the person in trouble?

2. According to this passage, what should my attitude be toward the person in trouble?

3. What is one specific thing I can do as a result of reading this passage?

Session 10

Cancer. AIDS. Leukemia. Cystic fibrosis. Despite the scientific advances of our day, these diseases and many others still plague us. It is a shock to hear that a person in the prime of life is doomed to die—and often headed for a lingering, painful death.

How can you help your kids deal with the terminal illness of a group member, church member, or friend? They may not want to deal with the dying person—nor even to think about him or her. Change that if you can, because such diseases create great need and great opportunity. We can learn much about life from the dying. Those on death's doorstep seem to have priorities that the rest of us have forgotten.

There's no question about it: Terminal illness is a tragedy. But if you are sensitive to the kids in your group, this session could be an eye-opener—as well as a heart-opener.

Crisis #10: Terminal Illness

Specific Aim

- To help kids understand that anyone suffering from a terminal illness is in need of encouragement and reassurance; to help them find ways to meet these needs; and to help them voice their feelings and develop more of an eternal perspective.

Scriptural Support

- Job 1:21, 22; 2:9, 10; 40:1-8
- Psalms 6:1-9; 22:1, 2, 12-24
- Isaiah 38:1-6, 10-20; 53:4-10
- John 9:1-5
- Romans 8:18-23, 28, 35, 37; 11:33-36
- II Corinthians 12:7-10
- Philippians 1:19-26

Special Preparation

- Bibles
- Copies of Student Sheet 10-A ("Tough Questions")
- Copies of Student Sheet 10-B ("Borrowed Time")
- Pencils
- Chalkboard and chalk or newsprint and marker

1 A Mind Trip

If someone in your group is facing a terminal illness, your kids probably already know the situation. You may have to explain the illness, to relieve confusion. If possible, describe the nature of the illness. Explain how long the person is expected to live. Talk about chances for recovery, pain, debilitation, etc. And focus on how the victim is taking this. [NOTE: This session probably would be most appropriate if the terminally ill person is not present.]

Say: **Imagine for a few minutes that you are in a hospital clinic. For several weeks you've had recurring cold symptoms. You've tried every household remedy, but just can't shake it.**

You've been in the clinic for three days, undergoing all kinds of tests. Suddenly your doctor walks into your hospital room with your parents. They are obviously upset. He calls you by name and says he has some very serious news. "The tests indicate that you have Acquired Immunity Deficiency Syndrome, AIDS. You may have contracted it from the blood transfusion you had last year. Although it's not yet full-blown, experience has shown that it's only a matter of time."

Pause to let everyone picture the scenario.

The doctor continues: "You probably know that there isn't yet a cure for AIDS, but researchers are getting closer every day. You have a better chance of surviving this illness than people did just a few years ago.

"The important thing is to try to continue to go about life as normally as you can. You're going to face some real fears. We'll do what we can, medically, but I suggest that you find someone to talk to." He gives you a business card with a counseling service name and phone number.

Your mother is upset. She begins to cry. Your dad seems angry.

Pause again as the group imagines this scenario.

Ask: **What feelings did you experience just now?** Jot down responses on the board.

What questions would you have?

What would be the first thing that you'd want to do when you got out of the hospital?

2 How Do You Feel?

Write the following four partial sentences on the board (or just say them aloud). Ask each group member to choose one, think about it, and finish the sentence.

- When I think about terminal illness, I feel scared because . . .
- When I think about terminal illness, I feel angry because . . .
- When I think about terminal illness, I feel sad because . . .
- When I think about terminal illness, I feel uncomfortable because . . .

After a minute or two, ask each group member to share how he or she completed one of the sentences. Complete one yourself to get group members started. Assure kids that all of these are understandable emotions.

You may find that your kids are scared about their own mortality. They may be angry at God for apparently afflicting this innocent person. They may just be very sad because they'll be losing a friend. They may feel uncomfortable because the disease grosses them out, or they don't know how to treat their friend.

3 Tough Questions

Hand out Student Sheet 10-A ("Tough Questions"). Explain that this worksheet deals with some tough questions that the group may have. Scripture helps us to deal with them, though there are no easy answers.

Divide into three groups. Have the groups read the assigned texts one by one, and see if there are any clues that might answer the questions listed. Have them write their insights in the space under each question. Explain that this is not easy—they may have to think a little. After several minutes, bring the groups together and go through the questions one by one. Use the following information to supplement your discussion.

Question 1—Why doesn't God work a miracle and heal this person? (Sometimes He does. With the blind man [John 9] and Hezekiah [Isaiah 38], He did. But sometimes He may want to allow us to be "weak" so that we learn to depend on Him more [II Corinthians 12]. And though physical death is sad, for the Christian it is a departure to a better life "with Christ" [Philippians 1].)

Question 2—Why does God allow this pain and suffering? (Who knows? That's the message of Romans 11—we just don't know all of God's plans. We do know that He joins with us in suffering [Isaiah 53]. It does enable Him to show His grace [II Corinthians 12] and love [Romans 8]. And it can work for His glory [John 9]. It still hurts, though [Psalm 22].)

Question 3—Is this God's way of punishing people? (Not necessarily. Jesus challenged that assumption in John 9. It is also apparent in many of the chapters of Job. In a general way, disease is a result of human sin. Romans 8:18-23 explains that we are temporarily in bondage to decay, but we await the fullness of our redemption.)

[NOTE: Use the following information with your group as needed. Some say that AIDS and other sexually transmitted diseases are punishments for sexual promiscuity. The rampant promiscuity of our society has created a climate in which such diseases spread rapidly. Usually, sin brings its own punishment. That is, the natural results of our sinning lead to disaster. We see that here. Our society has plunged so deeply into sexual sin, that many seem unable to be chaste—even at the risk of a deadly disease.

But it's hard to say that AIDS is an individual punishment. Many people are sexually wanton and still disease-free. And some are sexually innocent and have contracted the disease through blood transfusions (or from their spouses or parents). And, in any case, our response to someone with AIDS must be care and mercy, not judgment.]

Question 4: What sort of attitude should we have toward terminal illness? (Acceptance [Job 1–2], prayer [Psalm 6], humility [II Corinthians 12], praise to God [Romans 11; Psalm 22]. Basically, God says, "I'm in charge here. I'll run things the way I want. Trust Me. They'll turn out all right for you" [Romans 8:28; Job 40]. Still, God listens to and cares about our negative feelings, as He did the psalmist's.)

4 Borrowed Time

Hand out Student Sheet 10-B ("Borrowed Time"). Have a few group members alternate reading it aloud.

Then ask: **What does the author feel for his dying friends?** (Love, confusion, fear, etc.)

Why do you think he wants to avoid them? (They remind him that someday he will die, too; he may not know what to say to them; he thinks saying goodbye will be harder if he's close to them.)

Have you thought more about heaven and eternal life since you've been aware of __________'s terminal illness?

What sort of things might a friend suffering from terminal illness be able to teach us? (Joy in the midst of trouble and pain; how to live a full life, etc.)

How might an "eternal perspective" change the way we live our lives?

If a terminally ill person is not a Christian, do you think he or she might be more or less willing to listen to the Gospel at this difficult time?

5 So What?

Talk with the group about specific things they might do as a result of this session. They might consider: (1) a way of physically helping sick people; (2) a way of spiritually helping sick people; (3) a way of changing their own lives toward a more eternal perspective. Challenge each group member to come up with one specific action.

Close the session in prayer, asking for healing perhaps, for God's glory, for His comfort, for His grace.

Tough Questions

1. Why doesn't God work a miracle and heal this person?

2. Why does God allow this pain and suffering?

3. Is this God's way of punishing people?

4. What sort of attitude should we have toward terminal illness?

Group A
John 9:1-5
Isaiah 38:1-6, 10-20
Philippians 1:19-26
Romans 8:18-23

Group B
Psalm 6:1-9
Isaiah 53:4-10
Job 40:1-8
Romans 8:28, 35, 37

Group C
Romans 11:33-36
II Corinthians 12:7-10
Job 1:21, 22; 2:9, 10
Psalm 22:1, 2, 12-24

Borrowed Time

As I write this, my grandmother is 94 years old. She is a delight, witty and relatively healthy. I know she will not live much longer, and it doesn't bother me much. I will miss her, but she has lived a long, productive life—and when she goes, she will be with Jesus. Meanwhile, I enjoy talking with her. She is a link with the past.

Several years ago, I worked one summer with a young woman I'll call Peggie. She had cystic fibrosis, a disease of the lungs that claims the lives of most of its victims in their childhood. Peggie had made it to age 20 and was determined to break all records for surviving CF. She was one of the most cheerful people I have ever known. She would cough loudly, each cough a battle—but she emerged victorious again and again. The coughs grew more frequent as the summer progressed. But each new day was a gift that she unwrapped with glee.

Peggie's internship ended; she moved away. A year or so later, I received word that she had died.

Peggie changed me. I grew a lot that summer. I tore down some of my barriers.

And yet many barriers remain. In the last year I have learned that two friends have cancer. Both are beautiful, young women. They've had surgery and are currently doing all right, but they know they're living on borrowed time. The cancer will probably reappear. There are no guarantees.

To my shame, I must admit that I have avoided these two friends. I want to spare myself the pain of losing them, so I am not as close to them as I once was. I suppose I also feel something else—deep inside, where I can't understand it and can't really control it. To put it simply: Death grosses me out.

The idea that a friend of mine will die soon is an ugly thought. I don't want to deal with it. So, at a time when they need my friendship most, I am not there for them.

And yet, just as my grandmother is a link with the past, these two friends could be a link with the future. Peggie certainly was. Just by being there, she reminded me that this physical life is not all there is, that it will end sometime for all of us. Christians will live forever with God.

This "borrowed time" they're living is borrowed from God. And the fact is, all of us live on borrowed time. We have no guarantees. We could die tomorrow or next year or next century. In a way, all of us have a terminal disease—it's called life. Human life.

Death, decay, and disease—these subjects are avoided. Statistics tell us that many kids just ignore the AIDS epidemic, indulging themselves without a worry. They think it won't happen to them—that if they ignore it, it will go away.

But if we never think about death and our futures, we have no focus for our lives. It's like a photograph with no depth-of-field. It's flat. Each moment exists, but with no real reason to move on to the next moment. But if we know we have eternal life in Jesus, we can stare death in the face. And suddenly our whole lives develop a new texture. Each moment has meaning.

That's the sort of thing that Peggie began to teach me. I need to learn more.

— Randy Petersen

Session 11

Too often the headlines scream the news: A kid brings his father's gun to school and holds his classmates hostage. A drive-by shooting on city streets mows down innocent bystanders. A murderer stalks the women students of a community college. A car bomb makes a "statement" for a terrorist group—and kills a family.

We wish such tragedies would stay on our TV screens, where we could watch comfortably from our easy chairs. But they don't. Perhaps one has recently invaded your community.

People caught in such crises get angry at the perpetrators. And there may be some confusion about human nature and God's role in all of this. But the dominant emotion is fear. All the peace and safety people have taken for granted is up for grabs, and they're scared to death. Next time, it could be *their* corpses being carted away on the evening news.

Quoting the Shepherd's Psalm makes it seem so easy—"I will fear no evil, for You are with me." But we forget that in a dozen other psalms, the writer cries out against senseless violence, calling for punishment of the perpetrators and wondering aloud why God lets them get away with it.

God is with us, but that doesn't mean that violent incidents shouldn't shock us. It merely means that we can give our fear to Him, confident of His eternal protection. "Cast your cares on the Lord and He will sustain you" (Psalm 55:22a).

Crisis #11: Terrorism/Murder

Specific Aim

- To help kids deal with their anger and fear sparked by terrorism or murder; and to remind them of God's ultimate control of their destiny and the fleeting nature of this earthly life.

Scriptural Support

- Psalms 10; 23; 37:1-17; 52; 59; 64; 143;
- Romans 3:10-12; 8:38, 39; 12:19; 14:7, 8

Special Preparation

- Bibles
- Copies of Student Sheet 11-A ("Searching the Psalms")
- Copies of Student Sheet 11-B ("Tough Questions")
- Pencils
- Art, writing, and music supplies

1 Recall a Crisis

If a murder or terrorist incident has led you to use this session, invite the kids to talk about the incident. Strive for an informal discussion. Ask who was involved and what the group heard.

If there hasn't been such an incident, remind everyone of the Persian Gulf war of 1991. Ask: **Remember the Persian Gulf war? Have you ever wondered how it must have felt to be in Israel when Iraq was tossing Scud missiles their way? What words would you use to describe how it must have felt?** Write group members' suggestions on the board.

If a specific crime led you to use this session, ask: **What bothers you most about this incident?**

If you could say something to the people/person who did this, what would it be?

2 Expressing the Psalms

Say something like: **Sometimes people think the Bible is too ancient to have anything to do with modern life. Keep in mind that terrorism and murder have been a part of man's existence throughout history. Maybe that's one reason that the Book of Psalms is full of descriptions of a range of emotions that can help us express what we feel.**

Ask someone to read Psalm 23. Ask volunteers to suggest words that they would use to describe the feelings that the psalm elicits. (Suggestions might include peaceful, comforting, secure, etc.).

Ask someone else to read Psalm 10:1-4. Ask the group to suggest words that describe the feelings brought on by this psalm. (Fear, anger, confusion, etc.)

Divide into five groups. Assign one of the following psalms and the task beside it to each group (or person, if your group is small):

Group 1—Psalm 10—Create an art montage depicting the message.
Group 2—Psalm 52—Create a skit depicting the message.
Group 3—Psalm 59—Create a rap depicting the message.
Group 4—Psalm 64—Create a poster depicting the message.
Group 5—Psalm 143—Create a modern paraphrase depicting the message.

You may want to appoint a leader for each group. You might suggest that the groups select a verse or two at the heart of the psalm to concentrate on. Urge everyone to dig into the psalm's emotions. You will need to have plenty of art, music, and writing supplies available.

Give the group 10-15 minutes to work; then have each small group present its works to the group. Where possible, relate the feelings and events of the psalm to the incidents that have prompted this session, and the kids' current feelings.

3 Searching the Psalms

Hand out Student Sheet 11-A ("Searching the Psalms"), which lists the same five psalms that the groups just worked on. Explain that you're now going to study the passages more closely. Instruct each of the five groups to answer the questions for its assigned passage.

After a few minutes, bring the groups together for a brief discussion. Ask each of the questions on the student sheet, one at a time. Note the similarities in the five passages.

Point out that, in general, each passage shows the psalmist beset by evil, violent people. He is usually angry, and calls on God to take revenge. This is sometimes associated with an expression of trust in God—God is great and faithful and will care for us and destroy our foes. But sometimes the psalmist worries about whether God will act to save him. A crucial question is *when.*

Say something like: **It would be nice to think that God punishes violent evildoers right away, and that we will always be protected from physical harm. But it doesn't always work that way. Christians get killed by terrorists, too. But God's protection is long-term, lasting into eternity. He assures us that He will care for us forever. The murderers and terrorists may get away with their crimes for now, but eventually they will have to answer to God.**

Ask: **How can the psalmist be so angry? Aren't we supposed to forgive those who do us wrong?** Allow time for several volunteers to offer their opinions. Then use the following information to discuss your questions.

First, the psalms present a range of emotions. These are extremely honest, natural human responses to surrounding events. Generally, the psalmist ends up giving these feelings to God—that's why he's writing the psalm! We don't need to feel guilty if we respond momentarily with angry, vengeful feelings—but we should give these feelings to God, and let Him take care of them.

Second, revenge belongs to God (Romans 12:19). We have no right to take vengeance against sin, because we are sinners, too. But God is holy. The psalmist is calling on God to let His holiness be made known, and to crack down on sin. The psalmist is not taking revenge on his own.

Third, Jesus opened a whole new way of forgiveness for us. The idea of forgiveness was present in the Old Testament, but it was Jesus who radically demonstrated it. Because Jesus lives in us, we can share in God's feelings. That means we can hate sin, as God does, but also love the sinners, as God also does. We need to face violent crimes with both attitudes.

4 Tough Questions

Hand out Student Sheet 11-B ("Tough Questions"). Give each person time to complete the worksheet. Then ask volunteers to share their answers to each question. Use the following information to supplement group members' responses.

How can people be so cruel? (Sin. Human beings have rebelled against God. They need to know Jesus.)

What is happening to this world? Is it out of control? (God is still in control. He may allow strange things to happen, but nothing can keep Him from loving us.)

Why was I spared? (God has plans for us. Our lives are in His hands.)

5 Wrapping Up

Say something like: **There are many tough questions that plague us at a time like this. But God keeps saying to us, "Keep calm. Trust Me. I will take care of you." In closing, let's hear His words in Psalm 37. Take these into your heart and think about them.**

Ask a group member to read aloud Psalm 37:1-17.

Close in prayer, thanking God for His protection, and asking for His help as you seek to live full lives in a dangerous world.

Searching the Psalms

Scripture passages for study:

Psalm 10
Psalm 52
Psalm 59
Psalm 64
Psalm 143

Scripture passage assigned: ____________________

1. What seems to be the problem in this psalm?

2. What is the psalmist's attitude?

3. How are the wicked people described?

4. Who will avenge the crimes of the wicked?

5. When will God act to save His people?

6. What is the psalmist planning to do—or what does the psalmist urge the readers to do?

Tough Questions

1. How can people be so cruel?
A passage that may help: Romans 3:10-12.

2. What is happening to this world? Is it out of control?
A passage that may help: Romans 8:38, 39.

3. Why was I spared?
A passage that may help: Romans 14:7, 8.

Session 12

What do kids care about the economy? Plenty. Oh, they may not know much about interest rates and the GNP, but economic issues affect their families, and their families' finances affect them.

Will they be able to afford college? Will they be able to get summer jobs? Will they be able to buy new shoes? Fears abound. In tight times we also realize how materialistic we are, how much we depend on money.

Be sensitive to the emotional plight of your group members. And remind them that Jesus frequently warned against the dangers of money. It enslaves us, entices us away from God.

Maybe in lean times we can see things more clearly. As bleak as the current situation may be, it may give your group an opportunity to get closer to God.

Crisis #12: Economic Depression

Specific Aims

• To assure group members that God will provide for their needs; and to re-examine the role of money and material things in our lives.

Scriptural Support

• Matthew 6:19-21, 24-27, 31-34
• Luke 6:20-26

Special Preparation

• Bibles
• Copies of Student Sheet 12-A ("Sweepstakes")
• Copies of Student Sheet 12-B ("Treasure")
• Pencils
• Index cards

1 Congratulations!

Hand out Student Sheet 12-A ("Sweepstakes"). Give group members five minutes or so to fill it out.

When everyone is finished, ask: **Was it fun thinking about what you would do with all that money? How did you decide what to spend it on?**

Ask volunteers to share some of their expenditures.

Then ask: **What effect do you think this money would have on your life and relationships? Why?** If no one mentions it, point out that money can get in the way of relationships. As a tool, it can be used to help people, to show love. But it can also be used as a weapon. And, Scripture warns us, it can begin to dominate our lives.

2 Keeping Up with the Joneses

Say something like: **There are stories of lottery winners whose lives have been destroyed by their winnings. They usually go something like this.**

Jack and Evelyn Jones are a nice couple. He works in a factory; she works as a secretary. They win a lottery jackpot of four kazillion dollars. They're on TV. They celebrate. Then what?

They quit their jobs, of course. They move to a wealthy area in the next county. So, right away, they have removed themselves from the friendship of their neighbors and coworkers. But it doesn't matter, because *everyone* is very nice to them now. They get calls from relatives they didn't know they had. Every one seems to have medical bills or starving children. They help some, and never hear from the people again. The people they refuse get mad, and spread the word that the Joneses are snobs, now that they're rich.

Some friends from their old neighborhood drop by—just to be friendly—but suddenly the Joneses are suspicious. They think everyone is after their money. So they do become snobs.

They buy a lot of beautiful things for their house. But they have to put up a security system to keep people from breaking in, which makes them feel like they're in a fortress. So they begin to travel, doing all the things they always dreamed of. Everywhere there are new experiences to be had. They both end up having affairs, which destroys their marriage. They divorce, paying lawyers big bucks to fight over their fortune. They sell the house and divide the earnings. Then they settle into their individual lives—old and lonely.

Ask: **Is this story realistic? Have you ever heard similar stories?**

Why do people seem to lose everything after they "gain" everything—by the world's standards? (They often feel self-sufficient. They think they don't need others or God.)

3 The Blessing of Poverty

Ask group members to turn to Luke 6. Have someone read aloud verse 20. Ask: **What do you think Jesus meant by this?** Get some of their ideas and go back and read verses 20-26.

Why is it "blessed" to be poor? Is Jesus really saying it is better to be poor than to be rich? (The logic here is that, when this world treats us well, we have less of a desire for the next world. The coming "kingdom of God" belongs to those who are not shareholders in the kingdoms of this world. When we are comfortable in this life, we have less of a need to depend on God.)

Ask: **How does this make you feel? Does it surprise you? Does it make you feel better about the way the economy is, or does it make you feel guilty for having as much as you do? How do you think most Christians react to these verses?**

4 The Bible and Money

Hand out Student Sheet 12-B ("Treasure"). Divide into four groups. Assign each group one of the four passages for study. After several minutes, bring the groups back together for discussion. Go over the questions and get each group's responses.

Explain that the passages tell us not to depend too much on money or material things, and not to worry about our material needs. God will supply what we need—if He becomes our "Master," our top priority.

Money and material things are shown as (A) indications of where our hearts are; (B) capable of enslaving us and keeping us from full devotion to God; (C) not worth worrying about; (D) "extras" that God supplies.

Money and material things can distract us from serving God and keep us from trusting Him fully. This may explain why the poor are called "blessed." They get to trust God for everything. They are not distracted from following the Lord.

Don't field the answers to #6 publicly, but give the kids a few minutes to evaluate themselves and determine what their top priorities are.

5 So What?

Say something like: **It's all well and good to say that God will supply our needs, but how does He do this?** (Sometimes in miraculous ways, but also through His people, the church. That means that we must be sensitive to each other's needs and give freely when necessary.)

Does this mean that people whose families have a lot of money should feel guilty? If no one mentions it, point out that the Bible does not say it's wrong to have money. But it is wrong to love it, to trust it, to serve it. And the Bible often warns us that money attracts this kind of devotion. When you have some money, you want more. When you don't have it, you crave it. We expect money to solve our problems. The truth is that money is like fire, or electricity. We can use it to do a lot of good things, but it is also dangerous. It can burn us, or fry us. We should take care to use money for good purposes, and not to let it use us.

How should we deal with times of great financial need? Explain that, despite how difficult it sounds, the Bible says we shouldn't worry. Instead, we should trust God. And we should recognize that this may be God's way of bringing us closer to Him. We should be thankful for what God does provide. And we should take advantage of this opportunity for our faith to grow.

6 Saying "Thanks"

To close this session, remind everyone how fortunate most people in our society are, even in the midst of current troubles. Pass out a pencil and an index card to each person. Ask group members to write their own "thank You" notes to God. Encourage them to be as specific or as general as they want.

You may want to take the kids to your church's sanctuary and invite them to place their notes on the altar, in symbolic dedication to God. You may also want to invite anyone who wants to to share what he or she wrote with the rest of the group before placing it on the altar.

Before you close in prayer, ask for prayer requests about specific families in the church or community that are in need of help. Then ask God to provide for their needs, perhaps through your youth group and other Christians in the church. You may want to take an offering in the group now or in the near future to help with these needs.

SWEEPSTAKES

Congratulations!

You've just won the *Reader's Rejects* Sweepstakes! You will receive a cash award, after taxes, of $500,000.

How will you spend it? Please list the approximate amount you plan to spend on each of the following items. Feel free to add your own items as well.

Donation to church	__________
Car	__________
Bike	__________
Skateboard	__________
Home or home improvements for family	__________
Clothes	__________
Shoes	__________
Going out with friends	__________
Saving for college	__________
Saving for a "rainy day"	__________
Stereo system	__________
TV and VCR	__________
Phone bill	__________
Paying off parents' debts	__________
Take trips to exotic places	__________
Giving gifts to friends	__________
Other: ____________________	__________
Other: ____________________	__________
Other: ____________________	__________
TOTAL:	**$500,000.00**

Now please answer a few questions for our research files.

1. After receiving this money, how do you think you will feel?

❑ A lot happier ❑ About the same
❑ A little happier ❑ Less happy

Why? ____

____

2. Do you think your relationships with friends will be better once you have this money?

❑ A lot better ❑ About the same
❑ A little better ❑ Worse

Why? ____

____

3. Do you think your relationship with God will be better after you receive this money?

❑ A lot better ❑ About the same
❑ A little better ❑ Worse

Why? ____

____

Oops! We're terribly sorry, but we have just discovered a clerical error. You will not be receiving the $500,000 after all. But, to compensate for your trouble, we can offer you a subscription to *Reader's Rejects* magazine for the low, low discount price of $49.95. Save $500 off the cover price! Act now! Don't delay! This is your great opportunity. . . .

Treasure

Scripture Passages
A. Matthew 6:19-21
B. Matthew 6:24
C. Matthew 6:25-27
D. Matthew 6:31-34

Assigned Passage: ____________________

1. How would you sum up this passage in one sentence of ten words or fewer?

2. What does this passage tell us to do or not to do?

3. What does this passage teach us about money or material things?

4. According to this passage, how can money affect our relationship with God?

5. Does this passage help us understand why Jesus calls poor people "blessed"? How?

6. Consider these questions on your own:

   A. Where is your "treasure" stored?

   B. Who (or what) is your Master?

   C. What are you worrying about?

   D. What are you "seeking first"?

Session 13

Wars and rumors of wars. The rumors fly nightly on the evening news. The Middle East, South Africa, Ireland, Central America. Civil unrest in some foreign capital can quickly escalate to international proportions. The shock waves hit the whole society—including your kids.

On the national level, we might be talking about riots in a city or on a major college campus, perhaps an assassination—anything that throws the nation into turmoil, insecurity, disarray. And kids can sense the confusion that fills a country's people during tough times.

The simple assurance of Scripture is this: God is in control. When the world is spinning crazily toward destruction, the Lord's plans are still in place. Though madmen may perform their atrocities for now, God will not be mocked forever. In this world and the next, He guides His people to safety and peace.

Crisis #13: National or International Incident

Specific Aim

• To assure group members that God is ultimately in control of everything; to help them deal with their feelings of fear and helplessness; and to urge them to pray for their leaders.

Scriptural Support

- Psalms 2; 20:6-8; 27:1-3; 33:16-20; 47:7-9; 94:1-7
- Matthew 8:23-27
- I Timothy 2:1, 2
- Revelation 19:11-16

Special Preparation

- Bibles
- Copies of Student Sheet 13-A ("Feelings Flowchart")
- Copies of Student Sheet 13-B ("Who's in Charge?")
- Pencils
- News clippings about recent incidents to discuss

1 WHOSE SIDE ARE YOU ON?

Draw an imaginary line along the floor. Explain that one end of the line represents "Our country should be involved." The other end of the line represents "Our country should not be involved." Name several international incidents that have recently occurred, or a single incident that may have led you to use this session. Give each person a chance to find a place along the line that best represents his or her view of how much the country should be involved in each incident. If a single crisis has not precipitated this meeting, use the following incidents and add some more recent ones to your list:

- Apartheid in South Africa
- Conflict in the Middle East
- The attempt of Soviet republics to break away from the Soviet Union
- The attempted democratic revolution in China.

Ask group members to supply some details about the incident(s). Make sure all the relevant facts are brought out. Bring any news clippings that may help, and read bits of these to the group. Ask for volunteers to voice their opinions about the incident(s).

Ask: **Who's right or wrong? How could peace be achieved?** Don't be afraid to draw out the various viewpoints your kids might have. Let them debate the issues, if necessary.

2 FEELINGS

Hand out Student Sheet 13-A ("Feelings Flowchart"). Ask group members to fill in the blanks with phrases that describe their feelings and ideas of how God can help them.

Give them a few minutes to work on the sheet; then discuss it. Ask volunteers to share their responses. Use the following to supplement discussion of your group members' responses:

Worry—We may have concerns about the future for ourselves or our loved ones. But if God is in control of our eternal existence, we have little reason to let our worry get out of control.

Anger—It is common to feel anger at the leaders who have pushed a nation into a needless war or who have allowed an incident to happen. It's important to analyze this anger and then to deal with it. Our course of action is: (a) to give it to God (it does no good to be mad at the person responsible; God will avenge); (b) to forgive (and to learn).

Helplessness—It is frustrating to see major events unfold and not be able to do a thing about them. First, we need to see if we truly are helpless. Can we do something to improve things? Second, we need to understand the power of prayer. We are not helpless if God is our help.

3 Who's in Charge?

Hand out Student Sheet 13-B ("Who's in Charge?"). Give everyone about five minutes to work on the first Scripture passage. Then talk it over.

Explain that Psalm 2 shows the nations of earth raging against God, and God laughing at them. All their ranting is useless—He is still in control. Granted, not every modern conflict is fought against God. But whenever national leaders act with greed, pride, or anger and move into battle, they are going against God. God remains secure and confident. Their rebellion will not last long, and He has eternity to deal with them.

Then ask group members to choose their second Scripture passage (or you could assign these). After three to five minutes, have them share their answers.

Explain that Psalms 20 and 33 show the folly of trusting in weapons for safety. It is much better to trust God. This is especially important if you're dealing with a war or the threat of war. Group members (like their elders) may disagree over the use of weapons and armies. Challenge the group to examine where its trust really lies.

Psalm 27 tells us how to react. We need not fear. His "light" is not only the light of guidance, showing us where to go, but also the light of perspective. We see the long range of eternity, so the threats of this life don't matter so much.

Move on to the third passage, giving everyone a few minutes to work. Then discuss responses. The theme here is that the Lord is in control. Whether the enemies are armies or natural elements, the Lord is ultimately victorious. With that assurance, we can ultimately remain calm.

4 How Long, O Lord?

Say something like: **These questions are not as easy as they seem. It is true that the Lord will ultimately be victorious over the evil people who are now causing problems for the earth. But in the meantime, a lot of bad stuff is happening. People are being hurt and killed needlessly. Why doesn't God do something now?**

Explain that the Bible addresses this frustration. Ask someone to read Psalm 94:1-7. Point out that God is aware of our needs, and He does help us—in small ways now, in great ways to come. But right now, it's a struggle all wrapped up in God's mysterious sense of timing. He is letting the evil of humanity work itself out, but someday He will answer in full force.

Say: **So if you are agonizing, saying, "How long, O Lord, how long?" you're not alone. But keep looking forward to His future victory.**

5 PASS THE PEACE

Ask someone to read I Timothy 2:1, 2. Ask: **If you were to put that in today's language, what would you say?** (Pray for the President and Congress, etc.)

Emphasize the tough decisions leaders have to make today. Because of their office, they deserve our prayers. We should put aside any political disagreements we may have, and ask God to guide their decisions.

Say something like: **Sometimes when people are under a lot of stress, what they need most is a human touch.**

Invite the group to share in a powerful worship experience: "The Peace Touch." You will approach one of the young people, and say, **May you know God's peace**, after which you'll give the person a hug. He or she may say the same to you in response.

After the two of you have "passed the peace," both of you will approach two different people, say the same phrase, and give them a hug. Everyone will continue to pass the peace in this fashion until the entire group has been affirmed.

Then close the session in prayer.

FEELINGS FLOWCHART

Fill in the blanks in the following "Flowchart" to identify your feelings.

I'm Afraid

______________________	______________________
What Worries Me?	How Can God Help Me?
______________________	______________________
What Else Worries Me?	How Can God Help Me?
______________________	______________________
What Else Worries Me?	How Can God Help Me?

I'm Angry

______________________	______________________
At Whom?	How Can God Help Me?
______________________	______________________
At Whom?	How Can God Help Me?
______________________	______________________
At Whom?	How Can God Help Me?

I Feel Helpless

______________________	______________________
How Can God Help Me?	How Can I Help Myself?
______________________	______________________
How Can God Help Me?	How Can I Help Myself?
______________________	______________________
How Can God Help Me?	How Can I Help Myself?

WHO'S IN CHARGE?

SCRIPTURE PASSAGE #1—PSALM 2

Some Background: This was a coronation psalm, celebrating the day that a new king took power in Israel.

1. Write a headline that describes the activity of verses 1 and 2.

2. Write a headline for verses 4-6.

3. How does God respond to the threat from the nations (see vs. 4)? Does this surprise you? Why does He respond in this way?

4. How might this passage help us deal with an international crisis, where various "kings of the earth" are waging war?

SCRIPTURE PASSAGE #2—YOUR CHOICE OF PSALM 20:6-8; PSALM 27:1-3; OR PSALM 33:16-20

Some Background: Horses and chariots were the major weapons of war in those days. Today we might say, "tanks and missles."

1. How would you describe the spirit of these verses?

2. What do these verses tell us about dealing with national or international crises?

3. In these verses, what does it mean to trust the Lord?

Scripture Passage #3—Your choice of Psalm 47:7-9; Matthew 8:23-27; or Revelation 19:11-16

Some Background: These three passages are set in three distinct periods: ancient Israel; Jesus' ministry; the end times. But the Lord mightily shows His authority in each period.

1. If you had to put the main point of this passage in a telegram of ten words or less, what would it be?

2. What is the Lord in charge of? How do His "subjects" respond to Him?

3. In light of this, how should we respond to national or international crises?

Session 14

One of the hardest things Jesus ever commanded us was to "turn the other cheek." For centuries, we have tried to find a way around that simple teaching. When you are victimized, you certainly don't want to set yourself up to be victimized again. You experience rage. You feel frightened. You resolve to get even.

If someone in your group or church is a recent crime victim, your young people may be feeling that rage, fright, and desire for revenge. From something as serious as a girl being raped to something as relatively trivial as someone vandalizing the church bus—the question looms: "What do I do with my anger? How can I be at peace?"

Amazingly, Jesus says that peace comes not from retaliation, but from forgiveness, from love, and from trust. He Himself absorbs the vengeance, so we need to bring our feelings to Him. Otherwise we will sink in a whirlpool of hate and violence. That's a valuable lesson for your group members to learn.

CRISIS #14: CRIME

Specific Aim

• To help group members identify and, in a biblical way, deal with the feelings they have when someone in the group is a victim of crime.

Scriptural Support

• Psalm 5
• Isaiah 53:3-9
• Matthew 5:38-46; 18:21-35
• Romans 12:17-21

Special Preparation

• Bibles
• Copies of Student Sheet 14-A ("Courses of Action")
• Copies of Student Sheet 14-B ("Righting Wrongs")
• Pencils

1 Voters

Announce that you are going to be dealing with the group's response to a recent crime, but that you don't want to talk about the crime in specific terms until later. Instead, through Bible study and some hypothetical situations, you'll develop a general response to such cases, and at the end you'll talk about specific actions and attitudes.

[NOTE: This approach may also help you deal obliquely with the situation of rape. Some say the victim of rape is assaulted twice, first by the rapist and then by society, as her sexual privacy is paraded in public. You'll want to avoid this. In the case of rape, consider carefully whether you want to do this session at all. If you feel the kids really need it, consider whether the victim (if she's part of the group) should be there. And even then, whether she's there or not, use such care and sensitivity that the kids guard her privacy as well. Avoid getting into all the painful details. The victim may need to do that at some point, but only with her family or a counselor or her closest friends.]

Ask your group members to vote on the following issues to show their feelings about the justice system. Explain that you are going to call out several statements, one at a time. If individuals agree with that statement, they should give a "thumbs up" sign. If they disagree, they should give a "thumbs down" sign. If they don't know, don't care, or aren't listening, they should cross their arms.

- **I support capital punishment (the death penalty) for people convicted of violent crimes—rape, murder, etc.**
- **I support capital punishment only for people convicted of first-degree murder.**
- **I support capital punishment for teenagers who have committed murder.**
- **I support a life prison sentence for people convicted of violent crimes.**
- **I think our justice system is in need of a radical overhaul.**
- **I don't agree with everything that happens in our courts, but our system is better than any other system I know of.**

After each statement, ask volunteers to share why they voted as they did.

2 Case in Point

Hand out Student Sheet 14-A ("Courses of Action"). Explain that these case studies are hypothetical situations. Ask a volunteer to read aloud the first case study.

Then ask: **Should this person press charges in the interest of justice, or save his or her own skin and keep quiet?**

Help everyone understand the feelings that this person has after having been victimized. Ask: **How would you feel in this situation? What would you do?**

Have a volunteer read aloud Case Study #2.

Then ask: **Should this person take revenge, or let the guy go? Or should he do something *really* radical, like walking the guy home safely?**

Ask volunteers to explain how they would feel if they were the girl's boyfriend.

Ask: **Do you understand his anger?**

Do you understand the girl's desire to avoid confrontation?

What would you do?

Have a volunteer read aloud Case Study #3.

Ask: **Can you understand this person's feeling of humiliation?**

What should he do?

What do you think would happen if the person did pull out a gun in front of the muggers?

What would *you* do?

Explain that all of the cases offer basically four courses of action (which are not necessarily mutually exclusive):

(1) Taking matters into your own hands and avenging the crime;

(2) Going through the legal system;

(3) Ignoring it, avoiding confrontation;

(4) Finding a way to show God's love in some positive way.

Point out that there are pros and cons for each course of action. Vengeance is dangerous. It leads to more violence, and it goes against Christ's teaching. The legal system doesn't always work as it should. Ignoring feelings can allow emotional wounds to fester, unless they are brought to God. The fourth way, showing God's love, is ideal; but it is very, very hard to do, and can be dangerous, too.

3 LOVING ENEMIES

Hand out Student Sheet 14-B ("Righting Wrongs"). Give everyone a few minutes to work through the first section, then talk about it.

Explain that, in Psalm 5, the writer is angry. But he trusts God to deal with the evildoers. Point out that it is not wrong to be angry at those who do wrong, but that we should take these feelings to God.

Ask: **How do we take our feelings to God?** (Through prayer and trust.)

Say something like: **Let God remind you that He will make all things right in His own way, in His own time.**

Move on to the second section. Give group members a few minutes to study this on their own, and then discuss it.

Explain that the first debt mentioned is over a million dollars and the second is only a few dollars. The point is, we have all been forgiven for so much by God Himself, that we *must* forgive others. This is also summed up in the Lord's Prayer—"Forgive us our debts as we also have forgiven our debtors." We normally think of this forgiveness in terms of "minor" crimes, such as taking the last piece of cake or doing something to irritate someone else. But it must also apply to things like rape and robbery. Even these serious crimes are small compared to what God has forgiven us for.

As horrible as these crimes may be, we must see the perpetrators as people like us, people who need God's forgiveness. We might even be able to understand better how God reacts to our own sins.

Move on to the third section of the sheet. Give everyone a few minutes to consider the questions, then talk it over.

Say something like: **Believe it or not, we are to do good to those who do wrong to us. This will set us apart as Christians, and it may be more effective in bringing the criminal to admit his or her sin to God. It may take some creative thinking to find ways of showing this love, and it may take great courage to do so.**

One of the most difficult things to do is to forgive someone who doesn't want to be forgiven. And yet that is Christ's way. Remember, on the cross He prayed, "Father, forgive them, for they do not know what they are doing." So, to forgive a criminal who doesn't want to be forgiven is to follow Christ's example.

4 Wrapping Up

Say something like: **Let me tell you about someone else who was victimized.** Read Isaiah 53:3-9.

Ask: **Who is this talking about?** (Jesus, of course.) Point out that Christ was accused of crimes He did not commit. He was tortured, humiliated, and killed. He let Himself become a victim to win our salvation.

Say: **Many times, people who have been unjustly victimized wonder why they have been "singled out." They cry out, "Lord, how could You let this happen to me?!" It just doesn't make sense to them.**

But one of the best things you can say in a situation like that is that Jesus has been there. He knows what it's like. And, if nothing else, the experience can help us better understand the heart of Jesus, to share His pain, to reflect His love.

No, it's not wrong to feel angry or frustrated or humiliated. But these are just the first steps. Fix your attention on Jesus and let Him take you into forgiveness and love.

If appropriate, you may want to brainstorm specific ways to deal in a loving way with the recent crime(s). Otherwise, just close in prayer, asking God to help each person to come to a place of forgiveness and peace about this situation.

Courses of Action

Case Study #1

I was robbed. Walking in an unfamiliar part of the city, I was met by three large guys wearing gang jackets. They began teasing me at first. I tried to walk by them, but they stopped me. They wanted my money and my watch. When I realized that they wouldn't give in, I handed over my wallet and watch. I just felt so helpless.

I called the police as soon as I could, and reported the crime. The more I thought about it in the next few days, the angrier I got. I mean, it was wrong for those guys to do that. They had no right. It felt like I had given them a piece of myself with that wallet.

To my surprise, the police called back a few days later and said they had found my wallet. The money and watch were gone, but my license and a few other things were still there. The police had arrested the robbers on another charge, and were wondering if I wanted to press charges for the theft.

I wasn't sure. I mean, it was wrong for them to rob me. They should pay for it. But with our justice system, they'd probably be out on parole in a half hour. And I don't live very far from them. If I testified against them, they could easily find me and get back at me. And that scares me. What do you think I should do?

Case Study #2

My girlfriend was raped. She was walking home from work one night and this guy came out of a bar and started bothering her. Well, I won't go into details, but it was a terrible thing for her and her family. And I was angrier than I'd ever been before.

She decided not to go through the courts. She knew exactly who the guy was, but she just wanted everyone to forget the whole thing. The case was dropped.

Well, a year or so later, she was working late again. So she called me to walk her home. She doesn't walk anywhere alone anymore. We went by the same bar and, wouldn't you know, the same guy came out. He was pretty drunk, staggering a bit as he came in our direction. And I thought, "Here's my chance." I could beat him up and no one would ever know. I could make him pay for what he did. My girlfriend was pulling me away—she just wanted to avoid him, but I really wanted to hit him. What do you think I should have done?

Case Study #3

I was mugged on the subway a few months ago. There were these kids pushing people around, and they managed to corner me. They beat me up a little bit and took my money, which wasn't much. I felt humiliated. But what could I do? What I hate is that they were laughing the whole time. Like it was a big joke.

The worst thing is that I have to take the subway to get to my summer job. And I'm scared to death that it will happen again. Well, I've been thinking about it, and talking with some friends. One says I should get a gun and carry it with me. Then the next time some punks give me trouble, I should wave it around. It won't be funny then. Still, I'm kind of scared about that. What do you think?

RIGHTING WRONGS

GIVING IT TO GOD

Read Psalm 5 and answer the following questions.

1. How would you describe the psalmist's attitude? How does he feel toward the ones who have victimized him?

2. The Psalmist interweaves his hatred for evildoers (vs. 4-6, 9, 10) with his trust in God (vs. 1-3, 7, 8, 11, 12). Why is this significant?

3. In light of this passage, is it wrong to feel angry at or disgusted with those who have committed crimes against us or against those we care about?

4. What should we do with those feelings? How should we deal with them?

FORGIVING—AS WE ARE FORGIVEN

Read Matthew 18:21-35 and answer the following questions.

1. What is the main point in this parable?

2. Under normal circumstances, wouldn't the first servant be justified in demanding payment from his fellow servant? What made the difference?

3. How should this affect the way we respond to those who have committed crimes against us?

OVERCOMING EVIL WITH GOOD

Read Romans 12:17-21 and answer the following questions.

1. According to this passage, how should we treat those who do us wrong?

2. What effect do you think this will have? Read Matthew 5:38-46.

3. According to Jesus' teaching, how should we respond to those who do us wrong?

4. In what way can we "love our enemies"? What if they don't want to be forgiven? Does that change anything?

Session 15

You may recall the upsurge of interest in world hunger relief in the early 1980s. Tom Brokaw reported on the famine in Ethiopia and suddenly everyone wanted to help. The international Live Aid concert got musicians involved. Charities scrambled to collect and apportion the free-flowing funds. Hunger relief was "in."

There have been worse famines since then, but the world moved on to other crazes. Hunger continues to take its deadly toll, whether or not the camera is rolling.

Studies have shown that kids are concerned about hunger. They tend to have a strong sense of justice, and are bothered when life seems so unfair. Interestingly, one survey found that 52% of fifth graders considered hunger a major concern, but that figure dipped to 31% by ninth grade.

What happens in those intervening years? You can guess. Kids get more self-centered. They learn that their naive ideas of justice don't always work. And kids probably find their concern stifled, because adults fail to provide a good method to act on it. We just smile at their idealism.

Maybe you have selected this session because in your group there is a spark of interest about hunger. Great! Don't put it out. This session can fan it, fuel it, direct it.

CRISIS #15: WORLD HUNGER

Specific Aim

- To awaken kids to their responsibility to help the hungry; and to develop their desire to help in realistic ways.

Scriptural Support

- Genesis 2:9; 3:17, 18
- Deuteronomy 11:16, 17, 26-28
- Psalm 146:7
- Isaiah 9:6, 7; 58:6-11
- Matthew 25:34-46
- John 12:8
- Romans 8:18-23; 11:33
- Hebrews 2:14, 15
- I John 3:17, 18
- Revelation 21:4

Special Preparation

- Bibles
- Copies of Student Sheet 15-A ("The Big Picture")
- Copies of Student Sheet 15-B ("Responsibility and Reality")
- Pencils
- Chalkboard and chalk or newsprint and marker
- Prizes

1 Bible Drill

Start off the session with an old-fashioned Bible drill. Divide into teams.

Explain that you will call out a Scripture reference, which everyone will repeat out loud. When you say, **Go**, group members have to find that passage in their Bibles. The first person to stand and read the first word of the passage is the winner. Once the winner has been determined, have that person read the verse aloud.

Be ready with prizes, preferably edible ones. These might be small candy bars or, healthier yet, small bags of popcorn. It would be best to have many small prizes. After each verse, award a prize to the individual winner and everyone on his or her team.

At some point, you will need to choose an "oppressed" team, but keep this decision to yourself. In subtle ways, prevent this team from winning. Cheat. Make unreasonable demands. Dispute the wording of the verses. Change the rules. Move the team's best player to another team.

Use the following verses for the drill:

John 12:8	Psalm 107:9	Philippians 4:12
Romans 12:20	Luke 12:19	Mark 10:21
Matthew 6:24	Acts 2:45	Luke 19:26
I John 3:17	Isaiah 58:6, 7	Psalm 146:7

When the game is finished, allow the kids to begin enjoying their prizes. But take note of the one "oppressed" team—the team without any prizes.

Ask: **Do you winning teams think you should share some of your prizes with this team that has none? Why or why not?**

Play "devil's advocate" for both sides of the issue by pointing out the following facts:

- The winning teams earned their prizes, so they have a right to enjoy them.
- The game was "rigged" to hinder the "oppressed" team's chances.
- The winners shouldn't feel guilty for winning the game and enjoying the rewards.
- Since you're all friends in the group, you should share freely with each other. Besides, the winning teams have more prizes than they need.

Point out that the game you just played is somewhat like the world situation. In many ways, the world economy is a "game" that has lasted for centuries. Some countries are winning and others are losing. The same debate goes on. The "winning" countries argue that there is nothing wrong with their wealth; they have won it through hard work and ingenuity. But others point out that the rules are tilted in their favor. The poor countries don't have a chance. Besides, we're all in the same human "family"; we should share.

2 WHY IS THERE HUNGER?

Hand out Student Sheet 15-A ("The Big Picture"). Divide your group into four small groups. Assign each group one of the sections on the student sheet. After group members have had a chance to answer the questions for their section, examine them all, one at a time. Use the following information to supplement your discussion.

Group 1

What was God's original plan? See Genesis 2:9. (A world free from hunger, pain, death, and evil.)

What went wrong? See Genesis 3:17, 18. (Sin entered the world.)

What was God's role in famine and hunger concerning Israel? See Deuteronomy 11:16, 17, 26-28. (Throughout history, God told the Israelites how to live. "Do it My way," He said, "and things will turn out best for everyone. But if you don't, you will be cursed with famine and hunger.")

Group 2

What is God's plan for the end of time? See Revelation 21:4. (Same as the beginning—a world free from hunger, pain, death, and evil.)

How is He achieving His plan? See Isaiah 9:6, 7; Hebrews 2:14, 15. (Through Jesus, who has won the victory over the power of sin and death.)

So what happens in the meantime? See Romans 8:18-23. (We suffer and we wait and we groan.)

Group 3

OK, so God is going to make everything better for the poor and hungry at the end of time, but is He doing anything now? See Psalm 146:7. (Yes. He helps those in need.)

How? See Matthew 25:34-40. (Sometimes miraculously, like the manna from heaven or the loaves and fishes; but usually God works through His people. We are the "body of Christ" [Ephesians 4:15, 16] carrying on His ministry to the world.)

Group 4

Why doesn't God just work a miracle and give food to everyone? See Romans 11:33. If no one mentions it, point out that there are some things we just don't know about how God works. But we do know He has given us a challenge. Nowadays, He usually works His "miracles" through us, in ways that seem rather ordinary. In some ways, He's like the parent who takes the risk of letting his or her teenager drive. The trip may take longer or be more dangerous, but the kid needs to learn.

3 FOOD FOR THOUGHT

Hand out Student Sheet 15-B ("Responsibility and Reality"). Explain that you're going to take a closer look at our responsibilities as Christians. Assign Scriptures in the following manner:

- People born between January and April will study Isaiah 58:6-11.
- People born between May and August will study Matthew 25:41-46.
- People born between September and December will study I John 3:17, 18.

Give everyone a few minutes to answer the questions on the top section of the sheet. (The people studying the Isaiah passage may need to be told that "fasting" was a religious observance in that day; it had nothing to do with saving money to help the hungry; it was just a way of appearing religious.) Then have each group report.

Ask: **Do these verses indicate that true Christians will obey the Savior by caring for the needy?**

If we're not doing something to care for the needy, is there something wrong with our faith?

4 Get Real

Focus on the second section of Student Sheet 15-B. Give group members a few minutes to jot down their answers. Then ask for volunteers to share their responses.

Explain that the first question carries an important warning: If we expect to do away with world hunger, we will never totally succeed. Poverty, in some form, will always exist, until eternity erases all causes of sorrow. But we are still called to do His work, to help those in need. The commands of Scripture are clear, and they are not lessened by the seeming futility of the task. We may not erase poverty, but we may touch as many individual lives as we can.

The second question is more serious. The problem is that it sets up an either/or which the Bible does not contain. We should be doing both evangelism *and* hunger relief. And the history of Christian missions shows that evangelistic trails have often been blazed by those who have been doing some sort of physical ministry.

5 So What?

In closing, take some time to brainstorm ways that your group can address the problem of world hunger. Write group members' suggestions on the board.

Understandably, their personal resources are limited, but perhaps they could do a one-day fast or some other fundraising project. Perhaps they could launch an information campaign for the church, to keep hunger issues in front of the congregation. Perhaps they could begin to make lifestyle choices that will free up some funds for hunger relief (and develop habits that could last a lifetime).

Challenge each group member to follow through on at least one of the ideas.

Close in prayer, asking God to use your group members to help those who suffer from famine and hunger.

THE BIG PICTURE

GROUP 1

What was God's original plan? See Genesis 2:9.

What went wrong? See Genesis 3:17, 18.

What was God's role in famine and hunger concerning Israel? See Deuteronomy 11:16, 17, 26-28.

GROUP 2

What is God's plan for the end of time? See Revelation 21:4.

How is He achieving His plan? See Isaiah 9:6, 7; Hebrews 2:14, 15.

So what happens in the meantime? See Romans 8:18-23.

GROUP 3

OK, so God is going to make everything better for the poor and hungry at the end of time, but is He doing anything now? See Psalm 146:7.

How? See Matthew 25:34-40.

GROUP 4

Why doesn't God just work a miracle and give food to everyone? See Romans 11:33.

Responsibility and Reality

Part A

Scriptures: Isaiah 58:6-11
Matthew 25:41-46
I John 3:17, 18

Assigned Scripture: ____________________________

1. What does this passage say about those who claim to be religious but do nothing to help the poor or hungry?

2. What does this passage tell God's people to do?

3. Does this passage say what the result will be? If so, what is the result?

Part B

Scripture: John 12:8

1. Some people use this verse to say, "Since the poor will always be with us, what's the use of doing anything to help them?" Do you agree or disagree? How would you respond?

2. Some people use this verse to say, "Feeding the poor is obviously not as important as telling them about Jesus. So let's spend all our time in evangelism instead." Do you agree or disagree? How would you respond?